Panzer Division
the mailed fist

Panzer division
the mailed fist

Major K. J. Macksey, M.C.

Editor-in-Chief: Barrie Pitt
Art Director: Peter Dunbar

Military Consultant: Sir Basil Liddell Hart
Picture Editor: Robert Hunt

Design Assistants: Gibson/Marsh
Cover: Denis Piper
Research Assistant: Yvonne Marsh
Cartographer: Richard Natkiel
Special Drawings: John Batchelor

First printing: September 1968
Second printing: December 1969
Printed in the United States of America

Ballantine Books Inc.
101 Fifth Avenue, New York, NY 10003

Contents

Weapon of assault

Introduction by Barrie Pitt

Three decades after the outbreak of the Second World War, we are so familiar with mechanised vehicles both in warfare and in everyday life, that it is difficult for us to believe that shortly before the war began, important and intelligent commentators were prophecying that in it the horse would play a vital and possibly even decisive role.

Equally, hindsight renders it absurd that the few military planners whose imagination and foresight made them protaganists of armoured warfare should have been so unjustly treated – kicked variously upstairs, sideways, out, or simply ignored. A host of now famous names were victims in this ineptitude, notably the military consultant to this series Captain Sir Basil Liddell Hart, as well as Generals Fuller, Martel, Hobart, Broad, and Pile. In France, likewise, Charles de Gaulle planned for a tank war, and

was over-ridden.

But in Germany, the memory of the tank's devastating performances at the end of the First World War led to different conclusions. The tank, the Germans remembered, had played a vital part in forcing them into surrender in 1918, so twenty years later they had built up a tank force second to none – not numerically superior to the Allies, but stronger in technique, in doctrine, and vastly better endowed in morale.

Germany's Panzer Divisions were manned, in fact, by men picked for their exceptional qualities of physique and temperament, trained to a pitch of perfection, and imbued with a determination to revenge the shame of Versailles and restore the pride of the Fatherland. They were an élite of fighting men of a calibre matched only by their colleagues in the Luftwaffe.

In this book, which moves with the

speed and decisiveness of the Panzers themselves, Major Macksey tells the story of what happened when they went into action: how they raced across Northern Europe, ripped open Poland, the Low Countries, and France, pushed into Russia, and generally ran a merry massacre until, too advanced in their thinking and their efficiency, they over-extended themselves. They outran their lines of fuel and supply, and were in constant danger of being isolated from supporting arms of the German forces; and Hitler himself, startled at their speed of penetration into enemy territory, at one stage called them to a halt. He felt sure they were being drawn into a trap.

How the Panzers developed, how they took their place in Hitler's grand design, how their enemies were finally galvanised into countering them, is one of the fascinating stories of the Second World War. Above all it is the story of one of the great innovations in military technique.

Kenneth Macksey, author of *Afrika Korps*, one of the earlier books in this Ballantine series, is uniquely qualified to tell it. Himself until recently a serving officer in Britain's Royal Tank Regiment, he has written extensively on armoured warfare, including the history of his regiment.

In his hands the great battles in Europe, North Africa, and Russia spring to life once more, and the names of some of the war's great soldiers fill its pages – men like Guderian, Manstein, Rundstedt, and above all the 'desert fox' himself, Rommel. Their names are now part of recorded history. Every reader of this book will know why.

Secret birth

When 420 British tanks rolled out of the early morning mist covering the front line near Amiens, on 8th August, 1918, and broke through the German defences, the shock to the German Army of the First World War caused deeper repercussions than a mere penetration of the trench positions. In effect it struck a paralysing blow – of short but significant duration – to the brain of the German High Command. Yet this was not the first time attacking tanks had upset the equilibrium of the German infantry formations. It had happened during the British offensive at Cambrai in the previous November, and often, during the great offensives launched under the direction of General Ludendorff between March and July 1918, there had been instances of tanks breaking up German attacks and delivering ripostes which flung their infantry waves back to the gun lines. Until that morning in August, however, Ludendorff had chosen to dismiss the tank threat, putting his trust in massed artillery instead to open a way for strong infantry assaults employing infiltration tactics; and

on many occasions the subsequent disruption of the Allied Armies seemed to confirm his judgement.

Now the German Army recoiled and, by the truculent and mutinous behaviour of its soldiers, demonstrated that it could no longer be relied upon to carry on the war. Referring to 8th August as 'the Black Day of the German Army', Ludendorff impetuously proceeded to convince the Kaiser that the war must be ended; three months later, the defeated German Army was returning to a homeland wracked by revolution. Thereafter, the erstwhile military giant of Europe was reduced by the Treaty of Versailles to a maximum strength of 100,000 men and forbidden to possess offensive weapons such as bombers and tanks.

Thus two weapons, whose battlefield début had been performed less than five years before, figured in important clauses in the Peace Treaty and, in due course, injected strong provocation within a resentful German nation. The Versailles Treaty devised a political spur to those who wished to redress grievances in con-

Col. Lutz

nection with frontiers and pride: militarily it bred a desire amongst the soldiers to restore the honour of the German Army. So the search for restitution began in Germany – in the political field for a radical leadership, and in the military arena for methods which, should the opportunity arise, could be employed to conquer in a manner denied to the Army in the First World War. And since it appeared to the Germans that the tank had been a prime cause of their downfall, it was to the tank that they turned as one possible solution to their problems.

Without tanks of their own – indeed with very few mechanical vehicles of any sort in a predominantly horse and foot army, the addicts of mechanisation in the German Army could resort only to the use of theoretical and heavily simulated exercises to test their ideas. Within the law the most foresighted officers did all they could to learn new crafts, using whatever vehicles could be raised to practise motorised movement, making the men imitate tanks by pushing canvas screens before them, visiting those foreign armies which had tanks of their own, and reading every manual that could be found on the subject. Quite illegally, and therefore in deepest secrecy, they also designed and built two different tanks of their own – one light and one heavy machine – and indulged in a technical exchange with the Swedes and Russians that included the use of the Russian experimental camp at Kazan.

By 1930 a small élite of tank enthusiasts had grown up within the German Army – such men as Colonel Lutz and von Reichenau, and Majors Guderian and von Thoma, whose education in technical matters enabled them to grasp and put into practice a new military philosophy. Their ideas stemmed partly from original thought, but largely from studies of the methods envisaged by other nations – above all those being developed in Great Britain. There, an Experimental Mechanised Force consisting of tanks, armoured cars, and artillery and infantry carriers had exercised in 1927 and 1928, giving form to an idea which was then transcribed into an official pamphlet – and

soon faithfully translated for German readers. In Britain, too, General Fuller and Captain Liddell Hart, using the sort of language designed to spark off enthusiasm in young minds, expressed their belief in the prospects and the new methods that might be employed by mechanised forces. From these small beginnings, some of them almost lost from notice amidst the chorus of dissent that arose from soldiers whose minds did not readily accept the latent power of mechanised forces, there grew a new doctrine of war.

To only a very few did this doctrine appear in clearer definition than in the imagination of Heinz Guderian. In 1929 he became convinced that '. . . tanks working on their own or in conjunction with infantry could never achieve decisive importance. My historical studies, the exercises carried out in England, and our experiences with mock-ups had persuaded me that tanks would never be able to produce their full effect until the other weapons on whose support they must inevitably rely were brought up to their standard of speed and of cross-country performance. In such a formation of all arms, the tanks must play the primary role, the other weapons being subordinated to the requirements of the armour.' But only in the British Royal Tank Corps were similar views held to any extent, while throughout the rest of the British Army, the French Army, and all other armies – including that of Russia – tanks were kept subordinate to infantry as had been the practice in the First World War. There had to be a political upheaval, followed by a series of small demonstrations of tank power before Guderian's dreams could be translated into reality by the German Army.

In 1931 the British Tank Corps, under Brigadier Broad, manoeuvred in direct response to the will and voice of one man – the first practical display of radio control over an armoured formation. It introduced a new weapon to the battlefield since it made economies possible; for the exercise of personal command of a fighting body from the forefront of battle adds immensely to combat power, by ensuring the fullest co-ordination of

1. Col. Guderian
2. Col. von Reichenau
3. Maj. von Thoma
4. Gen. de Gaulle
5. Maj. Gen. Hobart

every weapon in the least possible time.

In 1933, when Adolf Hitler became German Chancellor, General von Blomberg was appointed War Minister and General von Reichenau was given the post of Chief of Ministerial Office. All three had minds that lay wide open to new ideas and, above all, to the potential of mechanised and tank warfare. Shown a motor-cycle platoon, an anti-tank platoon, a platoon of light tanks with some armoured cars working as a team, Hitler exclaimed: 'That's what I need'. At that moment, in effect, the German Armoured Force – or *Panzertrupper* – became certain of its destiny.

In 1934 the first German tank battalion, equipped with only a few light Mark I vehicles, whose design was founded on British Vickers models, formed at Ohrdruf. That same year the British, watched intently by observers from all over the world, exercised an armoured brigade of medium and light tanks and then combined them with a motorised infantry brigade in an all arms formation not dissimilar to that envisaged by Guderian. At the head of the British Tank Brigade was Brigadier Hobart, a dynamic soldier whose enthusiasm, thoughts and writings ran almost exactly parallel to Guderian's. But, just as the orthodox German soldiers resented and tried to curb Guderian, so did the British Army curb Hobart. Yet in Britain, as well as France, the USA, and, to a lesser degree Russia, the soldiers held fast to First World War concepts; but Guderian was enabled to develop his theories with the encouragement of Hitler and the more influential German armoured protagonists who had risen to the lead.

An armoured force and the habit of mobility (without which mechanisation becomes sterile), can only be created over a long period and as the result of much practical experience. In the 1930s there was no great pool of mechanically indoctrinated men to draw from in any nation, with the possible exception of the USA. Tanks themselves were also few in number, most armies having retained some from the previous war and restricted new construction to the manufacture of a few experimental vehicles. Specialised artillery and infantry carriers, along with other cross-country machines and suitable bridging equipment, were even scarcer. Germany possessed next to nothing except ideas and enthusiasm upon which to build a Panzer Army.

Men had to be recruited and trained, but suitable vehicles had first to be decided upon, designed, and then manufactured–a highly complex task that lay almost outside the experience and capability of German industry. In due course organisations had to be drawn up, tactics and a command system evolved – and with them the means to supply and maintain formations which were expected to move at speeds and cover distances which would far outstrip any manoeuvres previously achieved by other armies. A revolution such as this cannot be conducted in secrecy. Not only are the outward signs impossible to hide, but the thoughts that inculcate a new spirit and technology have to be disseminated by word and deed. When the volume of this indoctrination became widespread – as soon it did in the upsurge of German rearmament – the inhibitions imposed by the Versailles Treaty had to be thrown off. This Adolf Hitler proceeded to do, by inference, in March 1935, when he issued a Decree of Conscription.

The little Mark I tank which had performed to Hitler's satisfaction came into service solely for use as a training machine. In theory, its thin armour and lack of any armament other than two machine-guns denied it a place on the battlefield. Lutz and Guderian foresaw the need for two types of tank – a light one for reconnaissance and protection duties, and a medium one as the main battle machine. Realising that tank versus tank actions must, eventually, take place and that heavily armoured enemy tanks must sooner or later be met, Lutz asked for a high-velocity 50mm gun to be fitted in the PzKw3 medium tank, but had to be satisfied with a 37mm gun because that happened to be the type then being made for the infantry. For the medium PzKw4 tank, however, a 75mm gun with a low muzzle-velocity and the ability to fire high explosive as well as solid anti-tank shot was selected. In due course, as it happened, two medium tanks came into service and so three types, the light Mark II, with a 20mm gun, the Mark III with a 37mm gun, and the Mark IV with the short, low-velocity 75mm gun became standard equipment.

At first not one of these fighting vehicles carried armour more than 30mm thick – which exposed them to penetration by the 37mm and 47mm anti-tank guns then beginning to be adopted by most other armies. The German enthusiasts considered, however, that massed tanks moving constantly at speeds of up to 25 mph would, by distraction and pace, create inherent protection since the enemy would not be allowed sufficient time to concentrate against them.

It is one thing to lay down the specification of an armoured vehicle but quite another to convert it into a tank at the end of a factory line when the factory staff have never made anything like it before; and even the processes of manufacturing and joining the armour are a special art. Tank technology is a subject that takes many years to acquire and thrives on experiment, but in 1933 there were only a very few Germans with experience of a subject which, for lack of a civilian counterpart, calls for the development of processes at the frontiers of industrial knowledge. Furthermore, factories capable of making hundreds of tanks just did not exist. Therefore, before the new tanks could be given to the soldiers, there had to be a vast outlay on research and industrial expansion. For instance, the Mark III tank appeared as three distinct marks, each subject to numerous modifications, before a fourth mark – 'D' – went into limited production. Then only 55 of 'D' with its 37mm gun were made before being superseded by 'E' with the short 50mm gun – and even then Hitler's demand for a long 50mm had been ignored. For years to come the upgunning and up-armouring of the original tanks coincided with countless other improvements. Thus, it says much for the thoroughness of the original design that Mark IV, in its subsequent most highly developed state, was still in service in 1945 after six years of war. So, although criticism can be levelled at the early German design staffs for wasting too much time and effort on a host of experiments (which thereby slowed down the introduction of the badly needed new models), the end products demonstrated a highly economic durability.

In the final analysis it was the tank crews who made the German Panzer Force what it became, and so it is surprising what little attention has been paid by post-war German writers (above all the Generals) to the training lavished on those crews. Although the cadre came mainly from the 100,000 of the standing Wehrmacht, most of those who entered the Panzer schools, at places such as Wunstorf, came straight off the streets. But of the former, many were resistant to the new skills and mental attitude demanded of them: indeed, to be torn from the saddle and put into a driving seat came to some as an affront. Yet, from the beginning, the fanatical determination of leaders such as Guderian and Thoma entered into the souls of the first Panzer soldiers. The men were selected by merit, the quality of their aptitudes second only to that of members of the Luftwaffe with whom, in course of time, they were powerfully to combine. They felt and acted like an élite – and were given a special black uniform with a large, floppy black beret to distinguish their appearance.

An ideal arrangement in the training of a tank crew is to make each member learn the others' trades. There are three main trades – driver, gunner, and radio operator – the last in German medium tanks usually acting as the driver or front gunner as well. Over them all is set the commander who should be master of all trades and a tactician and leader as well. It takes time and great expense to train tank crews to the ideal standard, so quite often a man might learn only two of the three trades, or, if time did not permit, only one. The efficiency of the German Panzer soldiers when war broke out in 1939 stemmed from so many having learnt two trades or more, and by then, too, having gained much experience on exercises and during the bloodless coups on the periphery of the Father-

land. War, alone, could set the seal on that theoretical training.

But war was not in sight when the first of three Panzer divisions were formed on 15th October, 1935. No fighting formation in any other army in the world could boast of an establishment with two tank regiments each of two tank battalions numbering, between them, 561 tanks. A lorry-borne infantry brigade and strong motor-towed field and anti-tank artillery with engineers completed the all arms complement, but of heavy artillery there was none since that function was reserved to the Luftwaffe – above all to the dive-bombers which were to be introduced with the main purpose of blasting aside opposition to the mechanised army. In point of fact, the new Panzer divisions could barely be described as 'divisions' – let alone 'Panzer', for in 1935 only a trickle of the new Mark II tanks had begun to arrive and production Mark IIIs and IVs had not then left the factories! The paper organisation represented a framework within which Guderian (who had command of the 2nd Panzer Division) could build his dream of an all-armoured tracked force – though this largely remained a dream, for the Panzer divisions were never wholly tracked and far from being entirely armoured. It was the central core of tanks and armoured cars which gave Panzer divisions their title even though the towed artillery and lorried infantry (including motor-cyclists for scouting) were not armoured and only later, in some cases, tracked or semi-tracked.

As time went by and experience accrued, it seemed to the German General Staff that the infantry element in the Panzer divisions was too small in proportion to the armoured content. There were those, indeed, who desired tanks to be set specially aside to work, in the time-honoured manner, as escorts to the slow moving infantry assault, in much the way the French used their tanks. And so, in

1936, to Guderian's disgust, a Panzer regiment was told to practise this rôle, and at the same time the next three Panzer divisions, 4th, 5th, and 10th, were organised in 1938 and 1939 with a reinforced infantry element of four battalions, while the infantry in the original divisions was increased from two to three battalions. But this changed only in a matter of degree since it was agreed that, on many occasions, all arms combat teams or battle-groups could be formed within the Panzer divisions.

By 1937, however, the other arms of the German Army had become alarmed at the wholesale take-over being practised by the Panzer force. The Cavalry, concerned that they might be abolished, joined the new movement and got permission to create four so-called 'Light divisions', each of four motorised infantry battalions and a light tank battalion. At the same time the anti-tank companies allocated to work with the ordinary, marching infantry managed to obtain motor vehicles to draw their anti-tank guns – despite Guderian's plea that horse traction would be perfectly adequate.

The whole question of expansion depended, of course, upon the availability of equipment – above all of tanks and other mechanical vehicles. Realising that tanks were decisive but would always be in short supply by reason of production difficulties, if not from sheer expense, Guderian desired them to be kept concentrated. To him, dispersion of mechanical appliances to the Infantry and Light divisions merely diluted what little was available and reduced the inherent power of the Panzer divisions.

In fact, the formal Divisional Establishment Tables were never filled to capacity – and practice was to show that, in the field, loss by mechanical failures alone could whittle away 30% of a tank formation's strength even without the additional drain of battle casualties. Even before the Panzer divisions had fired their first shots in anger, their actual tank strength had shrunk to only 320; but before that much else was to happen of far greater importance.

Hitler re-militarised the Rhineland

Father of them all – the first Pz Kw I
Cardboard tanks for training.
The creation of armour –
the production line.

15

in 1936 – an exercise in political bluff that involved only a fraction of the ill-equipped Wehrmacht and not a single element of the Panzer force. By March 1937 he was ready to absorb Austria – but this time with a flamboyant *coup* involving strong forces, including the new 2nd Panzer Division. The whole affair – a bare-faced demonstration of outright power – had to be prepared in great haste and complete secrecy with the result that hardly any preparations could be made in advance and the units taking part had to be rushed towards the Austrian capital, Vienna, from starting points as far as 420 miles away. At that moment the training throughout 2nd Panzer Division had not reached a state that ensured it would operate as a cohesive formation. The tank crews were immature and had not even started company training: operational staffs were still learning routine tasks; there were no established supply columns (so the fighting vehicles could only be refuelled from depôts, local petrol stations, or by means of transport columns improvised by local civilian authorities); and the setting up of a Workshop Organisation had yet to be started.

Guderian, who had just been appointed General of Panzer Troops in succession to Lutz, led the advance to Vienna as commander of an improvised mobile XVI Army Corps comprising 2nd Panzer and the SS 'Leibstandarte Adolf Hitler' Motorised Regiment. He certainly had his problems, for apart from losing at least 30% of his tanks by breakdown, having to threaten a petrol depôt commander with violence in order to make him release his stocks, and tearing up the sole and newly laid road from Linz to Vienna with the tanks' tracks, he also earned the Army Commander's disapproval for festooning his tanks with decorations for the distraction and pleasure of the Austrian population. But to his immense satisfaction – and Hitler's apparent approval – the highly improvised journey made an overwhelming impression on all who witnessed it.

However, this was not combat experience. In 1937 that could best be acquired in Spain in the thick of the Civil War, and there Thoma found himself in command of a select body of German troops whose task it was to gain battle practice and help form and train the Fascist tank units of General Franco's army. No experiments with full-sized Panzer divisions could be carried out in Spain – the equipment just did not exist – but various other operational techniques, such as co-operation with aircraft and other combat elements, could be explored, while the technical defects of the light Mark I tank were ruthlessly exposed. In addition, Franco's tendency to disperse tanks thinly across the whole front met Thoma's determination to use them concentrated – and successfully – in miniature demonstrations of massive blows such as Guderian envisaged.

In the autumn of 1937 came the 'solution' of the Sudetenland problem when, at Munich, France and Britain agreed to allow Germany to take back the Sudetenland from Czechoslovakia without a shot being fired. And in March 1939, Hitler seized the rest of Czechoslovakia – this time without anybody's approval, for by now he sensed his strength – or thought he did. Throughout these hazardous adventures the leaders of the German Army boggled at the danger being run, for they considered they understood the extent of the military risks better than Hitler – even if they did not accurately calculate the dimensions of the political hazards.

On paper both the Wehrmacht and the Luftwaffe looked strong, although, in reality, both were weak in training and equipment. Only six Panzer divisions were in existence and these, in common with the rest of the armed services, possessed only a fraction of their entitled strength – least of all the really powerful new equipment essential to the maintenance of a credible performance at war. On 1st September, 1939, out of 3,195 German tanks, only 98 were Mark IIIs and 211 the powerful Mark IVs. Nevertheless, it should be remembered that, when taking over Czechoslovakia, no less than 469 Czech tanks fell into German hands along with the well advanced industrial establishments which had manufactured them. Before then the Wehr-

Hot from the production line – brand new Pz Kw IIs

macht and the Panzer force were paper armies, but after March 1939 they looked materially more formidable. Furthermore, out of success there grew a deadly confidence in the purpose and future foretold by Hitler, and with each bloodless take-over the reservations amongst the German General Staff faltered, partly because of being repeatedly proved wrong and partly because professional instincts were being whetted by the desire to try out what was being created. There can be little doubt that it was in the new, revolutionary arms, such as the Luftwaffe and the Panzer force, that an aggressive, experimental spirit arose most strongly.

In Germany the summer of 1939 lost its holiday atmosphere amidst intense political and martial activity. Hardly a week passed without Hitler demanding some new concession, or without the visit by a foreign dignitary, or some festive event, being used for celebration with a military spectacle to demonstrate the might of the German Armed Forces. At the centre of these parades would be seen the Panzer force, its columns of tanks driving as a phalanx down the Berlin Chaussées, or firing their guns in careful practice on the heathland ranges. Behind the outward show, deadly plans were being formulated and, when Memel was annexed and the war of nerves directed against Poland, there remained few in the know who did not understand that, soon, the demonstrations might give way to the real thing. And when, in August, the Anglo-French diplomats failed to make a non-aggression pact with Russia and, a week later, the Germans achieved that very aim, Poland's fate was virtually decided, leaving France and Britain with no alternative but to face the fact that they might have to declare war in support of Germany's eastern neighbour.

The Panzer phalanx on parade

Poland
The early trial

On paper and by the standards of 1918, the Polish Army looked as if it might have a faint chance with 30 infantry divisions and 11 cavalry brigades opposed to 40 German infantry divisions and only one cavalry brigade. But the presence of four German Motorised divisions, four Light divisions and seven Panzer divisions at various strengths, gave the Germans an offensive capability which the Poles could match only with one pitifully equipped, light armoured brigade. In the armies of the majority of nations, in 1939, the role of armoured formations was regarded either as an infantry adjunct, or as a sort of super horsed cavalry to be used as scouts, or in pursuit after a breach had been made in the enemy's lines. The Germans made no such nice distinctions. Panzer divisions were designed to fight in every phase of war, and at every opportunity, just so long as the ground would let them pass.

The Poles mobilised in seven major groups shielding their hinterland from incursions that might come from any direction along a common frontier with Germany of almost indefensible length. Mobilisation was never completed in full: their only real defence against tanks could come from a handful of field mounted anti-tank guns that lacked sufficient mobility to deal with a foe who worked in mass and at speed. Concrete fortifications might help impose delay in a few places – particularly in the more heavily defended sectors of the Danzig Corridor – and rivers formed useful barriers behind which fresh mobile defences might assemble. The balance of power, if it were to be restored to Poland, could only be altered by super-human bravery.

Fundamentally, the Germans stabbed two main pincers deep into the heart of Poland on 3rd September, with additional subsidiary prongs reaching outwards on either side of the main axes. Army Group North's Fourth Army struck eastwards out of Pomerania with the intention of cutting the Danzig Corridor, while its Third Army advanced southwards from East Prussia in the direction of Warsaw. Army Group South with,

Only a training machine – a Pz Kw I in action

23

The Polish campaign – 1939

The concentration of a professio...

from left to right, Eighth, Tenth and Fourteenth Armies, swept north-eastwards out of Silesia and Slovakia also in the direction of Warsaw, with its central thrust line passing north of Kraków. This grandiose scheme lacked nothing in ambition, while the proportion of Panzer divisions denoted in what sectors the German High Command intended to win the decision. Two of the six were in the north with XIX Army Corps, under Guderian, in Fourth Army, and the remainder in Army Group South with two in Hoeppner's XVI Corps of Tenth Army, ready to take the shortest route to Warsaw.

Panzer operations, however, were not necessarily designed to take the most obvious defended path, even though each physical assault might be direct and brusque. Where unavoidable opposition had to be overcome, such as the fortified zone met by Guderian's XIX Army Corps south of Danzig, it was hit by the shock of several waves of tanks spaced in echelon over a narrow front that hardly exceeded 5,000 yards in width. Ahead and to the flanks, dive-bombers and artillery fire pounded those artillery and anti-tank positions which might cause most harm to the tanks. In rear the lorry-borne infantry followed cautiously, anxious not to expose their unarmoured vehicles to direct fire. Hence nearly everything depended in the first instance upon the determination and effect of the tanks. When they met well posted and bravely served anti-tank guns they suffered heavy casualties and had either to destroy the guns with their own fire or work round a flank to bypass the opposition. But if the defenders blocked the only serviceable route, the tanks had to wait until the infantry could approach, dismount out of view, and deliver a formal attack covered by both artillery and tanks. Speed was the overriding factor in each Panzer attack – but if an attack could be averted by circumvention, the final outcome could be paralysing to the enemy. Unarmoured infantry merely hampered the pace of action.

On the first day Guderian, driving in an armoured vehicle with the leading troops of 3rd Panzer Division (the first senior commander ever actually to control a tank corps in the forefront of the battle from behind armour) came under heavy fire from his own heavy artillery even though the gunners had been told to withhold their fire. Later that day, when he found the leading troops had stopped at the River Brahe, even though the enemy defences were practically non-existent, he was to discover that there simply was no-one to lead and break the deadlock. German tanks and infantry were blazing away with indiscriminate fire against an invisible enemy, and only by his personal exertions did he manage to organise a crossing and send the tanks ahead once again. Most of the German Army lacked experience under fire, and so, for the first few days, it behaved in the manner of all 'green' troops. That is, it panicked at minor opposition and rumours, and then took far too long to overcome even the most trivial opposition.

The action on the Brahe was of the more deliberate kind. Thereafter, as the enemy began to crumble, Guderian's Corps sought to advance along routes considered, by the Poles, as impassable to tanks – straight through the thick Tuchola Forest instead of across open, so-called 'good' tank country towards Bydgoszcz. By 5th September the Danzig Corridor had been overrun and Fourth Army's Panzers had linked up with Third Army in East Prussia and were on their way to prepare a drive down the left flank of the Third Army. For the Third Army, unaided by tanks (except for those in an independent Panzer brigade), had run into trouble against the Polish defences and not made the

Lamb to the slaughter – a Polish tank of British origin awaits the Panzer Divisions

The irresistible onrush of the Panzers

same sort of dramatic progress as had been made elsewhere.

Army Group South, rich in armour, and under the command of General von Rundstedt and his Chief-of-Staff, General Manstein, sent Tenth Army half way to Warsaw in the same time as it had taken Fourth Army to overcome the Corridor. They too followed the line of least expectation, committing tanks to country where an enemy, taught to believe that tracked vehicles could not penetrate close country, had neglected to arrange defences against them. Thus, in Fourteenth Army, Thoma's Panzer brigade in 2nd Panzer Division was ordered, on Thoma's suggestion, to move through thick woods over a ridge instead of by the obvious way through the Jablunka Pass. The psychological effect of a blow such as this is described by Thoma himself: 'On descending into the valley I arrived in a village to find the people all going to church. How astonished they were to see my tanks appearing. I had turned the enemy's defences without losing a single tank – after a night approach march of 50 miles.' In

so doing he underlined a new principle: that a few tanks in the least obvious undefended spot are worth a mass at the most likely and best guarded locality.

On 3rd September, France and Britain, still not fully mobilised, had entered the war on Poland's side and, by 6th September, the Poles could delineate the course of the principal enemy thrusts. The Third and Fourth German Armies were approaching Warsaw along the north bank of the River Vistula, with Guderian's XIX Army Corps supplying its impetus with 3rd and 10th Panzer Divisions in a drive east of the River Bug, behind the main Polish lines, aimed at the route centre of Brest Litovsk. Runstedt's Army Group South, having swung up from the south against Warsaw, reached the line of the River Bzura after overcoming a succession of Polish lines of resistance, not one of which had been manned in time by the defenders whose whole concept of pace had been upset by the speed of the German attacks. The Vistula was reached by the Germans along almost its entire length: in hordes, Polish prisoners-of-war entered captivity. General List's Fourteenth Army, having broken through with 2nd Panzer Division in the lead, was turning east towards Lwow and, eventually, the line of the Bug. The whole front was in motion – nowhere could the Poles effect stability.

Indeed, only at one point did the Poles adopt the one policy that stood any chance of stopping the Panzers – a counterstroke of their own. To the west of Warsaw, from within becalmed territory that was being isolated by the northern and southern arms of the German envelopment, the Polish Poznan and Pomorz Armies saw the opportunity to strike a concentrated blow against the flank guard provided by VIII Army. For, at the very moment when the Germans were directing their whole attention to taking Warsaw, their Tenth Army had run short of fuel at the end of prolonged lines of communication. The attack by Poznan Army started on the morning of the 9th and achieved initial successes against the infantry formations of the German Eighth Army. Not until that evening, however, did the Germans appreciate the magnitude of the threat to their flank, but thereupon their reaction showed just how flexible Panzer and motorised divisions could be in defence.

It might be truer to say that the defensive battle fought by the German Army Group South at the Bzura was strictly offensive in nature. Unfortunately, for them, the Poles had made their counterattack on a narrow front in order to achieve a local initial superiority of force at the price of creating the conditions necessary to sustain action. Motorised divisions can be deflected on new fronts at great speed. In a matter of hours General von Richenau had achieved a deadly concentration on the southern boundary of the Poznan Army, while Runstedt brought in still more reinforcements from the north-west to catch the attackers in rear. And from Warsaw and the Vistula, 1st and 4th Panzer Divisions gave up probing the city's outer defences to swing back westward to help complete the rout of Poznan Army.

Indeed, 4th Panzer Division was glad to leave Warsaw alone. In trying to fight its way through the suburbs it had discovered that city streets, where scope for manoeuvre is inhibited and where there is only one line of approach, seriously reduced a tank formation's effect. Three hours' fighting on the 9th cost that division 57 out of 120 tanks engaged, and taught the Panzers a thorough lesson – but one nevertheless that they did not always remember in the future.

By the evening of 15th September, what few Poles remained in the Bzura pocket stood dazed amongst wrecked and blazing equipment in territory that had been subjected to an all-out assault by massed German divisions, efficiently supported by bombing attacks – only a few survivors escaped eastwards to join the defenders of Warsaw. Elsewhere attempts were being made to re-establish a front protecting the eastern half of the country and hopes of ultimate survival were buoyed up by a promise from the French that, on the 17th, they would launch a major assault into Western Germany – a venture which could have caused immense damage to the Germans since their frontier with France had been almost denuded of troops in order to conquer Poland. There was not a single Panzer division in the Fatherland and, with every gain in Poland, they moved rapidly further east. To switch a sizeable force – even a fast moving mechanised one – might have taken too long to ensure the safety of those German industrial centres close to the French border.

But the French hardly staged a demonstration, let alone an offensive; and, in any case, resistance in Poland practically ceased to have meaning when, on the 14th, Guderian's XIX Corps – made at this period into an 'ideal' Panzer corps comprising two Panzer and one Motorised division – encircled Brest Litovsk. At times even the Germans themselves ran into difficulties caused by the speed and complexities of their runaway progress. On the way to Brest Litovsk, bridges had to be built over the River Narew on the night of 9th September to carry 10th and 3rd Panzer Divisions to the southern bank. Next morning, Guderian discovered to his annoyance that the tanks were still on the northern bank because XX Motorised Division had dismantled the bridges during the night and taken them downstream for their own use. It was a straightforward error in staff work, but it delayed the advance by 24 hours and re-emphasised, what had long been known, that mechanised forces have few greater problems to overcome than that of crossing water obstacles. Guderian was mollified however, by an exploit in which some of his tanks caught and destroyed Polish tanks as they detrained in a siding.

Guderian arrived at Brest Litovsk on the 14th, but its citadel did not surrender until the 17th. By then, this ancient city was also the target for the southern German pincer when, to the surprise of the German soldiers, as much as the Poles, the Red Army crossed the eastern Polish frontier and proceeded to occupy the eastern half of the country. Warsaw continued to hold out, in a symbolic and hopeless resistance that lasted until 27th September, while scattered Polish parties fought at Kock until 6th October; but, as the Germans had already learnt, tanks are at a disadvantage in a great city, so their Panzer divisions played no great part in this last act of the campaign. They had been the source of victory. Now they could return to the Fatherland to refit and get ready to deal with any French counteroffensive that might develop.

In the meantime, the High Command had the task of considering the lessons of four weeks' combat and put right what was palpably wrong.

Of course, much had gone right for the Germans. The Panzer divisions had demonstrated immense power in the hands of men of sterling calibre. Command by the senior commanders from the van of the battle had shown that intervention at the vital point by somebody in possession of all the known facts whose attention was not rivetted to the immediate scene could lubricate the sort of battlefield friction of which Clausewitz had once written. More often than not, however, friction had been caused by the staff over whom the Higher Commanders ruled, and the reason for this lay within the realms of organisation and training; neither staffs nor communications had kept pace with the speed of the machines they were supposed to control, the more so since many of the staff lacked a sufficient appreciation of the technical problems posed by mechanisation.

Not even within the Panzer divisions themselves had everything gone right. Their basic tools, the tanks, had behaved well with only 25% falling out of action at any one time from mechanical failure, but at the end of the campaign every machine was badly in need of servicing. Tank casualties amounted to 217, mostly from enemy anti-tank guns which had taken their toll of the older, light machines. Of course, the conclusions to be drawn from this first major practical test had to be under-valued because the opposition had been so poorly equipped. On the other hand, this gradual and fairly gentle combat innoculation eased the long-term training programme by teaching the soldiers their basic skills at low cost. No full-blooded tank versus tank engagements had taken place, leaving the Panzer divisions to operate at a pace of their own choosing. Yet serious trouble arose when the tanks got out of touch with their supporting infantry: time and again the rifle regiments, held in rear by the need to keep their unarmoured vehicles out of harm's way, were too far back to intervene in time to assist the tanks, when immediate infantry action might have ensured the continual momentum. The co-operation of the Luftwaffe provided essential indirect help in sweeping the enemy air force from the sky and thereby permitting land movement to take place unimpeded by enemy aerial interdiction: in addition it did much to disrupt enemy rearward defences before the Panzer divisions reached them, helped spy out a lot of what went on behind the enemy lines, and provided commanders with aerial command posts. However, intimate aerial bombardment in the forward edge of the battle zone was not so well executed – and this was something that study and fresh training alone could put right.

Generally speaking, the Panzer

Light tank Pz Kw38t
The acquisition of Czechoslovakian tank production boosted the tank strength of the Panzer Divisions in 1939. 7th and 8th Panzer Divisions were largely equipped with the 38t in 1940 and found them a satisfactory fighting machine against the French and British. Later the chassis was used for many other purposes. Weight: 10 tons. Speed: 25 mph. Crew: four. 1 x 37mm gun and 2 x 7.9mm mg.

divisions had shown that pre-war planning, organisations, and methods were more than equal to the sort of defences erected by the out-dated conventional European Armies of the day. The Motorised Infantry divisions had acted as invaluable complements to the Panzer divisions – the grouping of one Motorised division, being compatible with two Panzer divisions grouped in a Panzer corps. The Light divisions had failed because they neither had enough tanks to allow them to work like a Panzer division, nor the right proportion of infantry for use as motorised or conventional infantry divisions. The marching Infantry divisions, with their horsed artillery and transport, had played the walking on part in an old fashioned lugubrious manner, and been severely criticised by the Field Commanders, when they ran into difficulties, for lack of initiative. Horsed cavalry had failed wherever it had come, unwisely, into action.

Poland lay prostrate – and the rest of the world, since it did not have full access to the evidence, could not judge the overriding reasons why. Knowing that the Polish Army had been seriously short of modern equipment, the French and British chose to assume that to be the prime cause of the rapid collapse – though the French took the tank lesson somewhat closer to heart by beginning to group some of their tanks into special *Divisions Cuirasée* (DCM). Generally speaking, however, the potency of the Panzers remained concealed to the West.

France
The designs
are sealed

Indoctrination of the West – Panzer in Norway

It might have been expected that the decisive role played by the Panzer divisions in the Polish Campaign would have convinced the main body of the German General Staff of the dominant power of armoured troops when thrown into combat against the conventional armies of the old order. In fact this was far from the case, largely because the more senior German officers had still to come to terms with the extra pace induced by mechanised warfare and also because a comparison between the relative strengths of the Polish Army and the combined Franco-British Army hardly bore examination. In any case, the Germans had a strong respect for French military skill. So, in parallel with Franco-British doubts concerning the efficiency of armoured formations, the Germans planned to invade Western Europe more or less along the lines of the First World War.

They projected an invasion with a strengthened right wing through the Low Countries in order to turn the fortified Maginot Line guarding France's eastern frontier, aiming to fall upon the flank and rear of the Allies in the manner of the old Schlieffen Plan of 1914. The Allies, on the assumption that this would be the essence of any German Plan – if only because the Maginot Line seemed to preclude an alternative, arranged to meet it with a reciprocal wheel that would stop the Germans in Belgium amongst a succession of defended river lines. The Allied Armies had already reached a comparatively high degree of mechanisation, and their tank strength was actually well in excess of the Germans; but from the organisational and employment aspects, their doctrine favoured the infantry/cavalry concepts, committing their tank divisions to be spread thinly across the front and their 'infantry' tanks to being scattered in small groups amongst the infantry formations. They did not seek concentration at any one point.

There were many amongst the German Commanders who had been so impressed by the Panzer divisions' performance in Poland that they

wished nothing better than to be associated with that arm. Amongst these was General Erwin Rommel – an infantryman who had commanded Hitler's personal escort in Poland. To Rommel's request for command of a Panzer division, Hitler responded by giving him the 7th – one of four (the 6th, 7th, 8th, and 9th) that were formed out of the unhappy Light divisions that had done so badly in September 1939. Preparations for a modernised Schlieffen Plan began immediately after the Polish Campaign, while the Panzer divisions themselves underwent as much re-equipment, reorganisation, and re-training as limited resources permitted. In the meantime, Rundstedt's Chief-of-Staff, Manstein, conceived a fresh way of breaking the French Front without recourse to the Schlieffen swing, making full use, instead, of the Panzers' ability to penetrate wild, so-called tank-proof terrain in the fashion demonstrated in Poland. Manstein dreamed on a great scale, proposing that the entire Panzer force – all ten divisions plus the motorised ones – should be launched through the forests and circumscribed roads of the Ardennes, to seize crossings over the River Meuse prior to striking out eastward past the lightly guarded flank of the Maginot Line.

Nothing could have pleased Guderian and the other tank enthusiasts more. The German High Command, however, exhibited considerable misgivings and wished to water down the scheme by using the Panzer divisions in several dispersed thrusts such as had been done in Poland. They adhered to their original plan, dropping it only after a courier accidentally delivered its entire contents into Allied hands after an air crash in Belgium. Manstein's persistence cost him his job as Chief-of-Staff to von Rundstedt, but, he still managed to convey the substance of his Ardennes plan to Hitler with the upshot that, by degrees, throughout a number of War Game Studies, it became the foundation of the German plan to invade the West. Holland was still to be attacked along with Belgium and Luxembourg, but mainly to give the impression that the

Schlieffen Plan remained in operation. In this way the best of the Allied mobile troops would be drawn into Belgium, away from the intended point of impact between Dinant and Sedan. For the decisive blow no less than ten Panzer and 34 other divisions were to be deployed from depth behind the Ardennes while the remainder of the German Army masked the Maginot Line or pushed into Holland and Belgium with infantry and air-born troops (aided at first by Schmidt's XXXIX and Hoeppner's XVI Panzer Corps). There were four Panzer corps: Hoeppner's XVI, Hoth's XV, and Reinhardt's XLI Panzer Corps, each with two Panzer divisions, and Guderian's XIX Panzer Corps with three Panzer divisions. A Motorised division also went with each Panzer corps, plus essential specialist assistance from bombers, heavy artillery and bridging equipment allocated to suit the special circumstances to be expected on each corps' front.

Two hazards dominated German fears before the operation. Could they force the Ardennes without becoming trapped in its environs by a relatively trivial French effort; and could they cross the Meuse without loss of momentum and enormous casualties? Guderian, not believing that anything could stop his progress through the Ardennes, allowed his thoughts to dwell more on what might be done after the crossings had been accomplished, and when Hitler – the only one to do so, asked what he would then do, he replied, 'Unless I receive orders to the contrary, I intend on the next day to continue my advance westwards. The supreme leadership must decide whether my objective is to be Amiens or Paris. In my opinion the correct course is to drive past Amiens to the English Channel'. Nobody contradicted him – partly because most doubted if the bridgehead would be created at all.

In tactical technique the Germans were far in advance of the Allies, but in tanks, the vital tools of an armoured breakthrough, they were deficient, despite the infusion of new but delayed production, and the acquisitions from Czechoslovakia. On 9th May 1940, the eve of the invasion, they only had 627 of the good Mark IIIs and IVs:

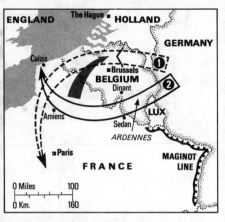

Plans of conquest –
Schlieffen 1 Manstein 2

The break-in at Sedan

the remaining 2,060 tanks, with the exception of 381 Czech 38ts armed with a 37mm gun, were the early Mark Is and IIs.

The French could muster about 3,000 tanks plus a great many obsolete machines in reserve formations. Of that 3,000, 1,292 were included in the Light Mechanised Divisions (DLM) and the *Divisions Cuirasée* (DCR): the remainder were split amongst the infantry formations. The British had 210 light tanks and 100 heavy 'Infantry' tanks in France, all committed to work with infantry, while a further 174 light and 156 cruisers belonging to their 1st (and only) Armoured Division waited shipment from Britain. The numerical odds were thus on the Allied side. Quality came out about equal. The best French tank, the Char B, mounted a good 47mm gun in a fully rotating turret and had a 75mm gun slung between the tracks. The 20-ton Somua also carried a 47mm in a turret and was fast as well. Armour thicknesses were between 40mm and 60mm compared with the 30mm used, at best, by the Germans. The British light tanks were as vulnerable as their German counterparts, but their 100 Infantry tanks (including 23 of the brand new Matildas) were covered by armour up to 70mm thick – quite proof against the German anti-tank guns – while the 2-pounder gun on the Matilda could penetrate any German tank at battle ranges.

Unhappily for the French, their policy of seating the tank commander in isolation in the turret, forcing him to carry out the commander's as well as the gunner's functions, led to a lowering of combat efficiency and a loss of control. The three-man turret adopted by the Germans and the British (except in their Mark I Infantry and light tanks) was a much better arrangement, and helped crews and formations to fight as properly integrated teams. Teamwork was the key to German superiority, for they insisted on their Generals taking charge at the front, in close contact with their men and the situation (with a consequent enhancement of morale). But the French and British started by applying control from headquarters too far in rear along communications of uncertain reliability, and the former had the habit of halting to receive orders, thus losing momentum in the process.

Germany had invaded Denmark and Norway on 9th April and within a month had swallowed both nations with the exception of a small enclave near Narvik in Norway. Tanks, but no Panzer divisions, played a small but significant role in these operations.

Breaking through

**The 88 –
anti-tank or anti-aircraft gun**

Water obstacles

Opening the breach – the Ardennes

88 in action. Knocked out French Char B alongside

Exploiting the breach

During the night of 9th/10th May the Germans began to operate against the Low Countries. Within four days a combined airborne and land assault had knocked out Holland and the Allies had swung into Belgium, according to plan, and were engaged with German troops along the line of the River Dyle. In the meantime the three Panzer divisions of XXXIX and XVI Panzer Corps had been in action – one in Holland and the two others at Gembloux and Hannut – while the other three corps threaded their way through the Ardennes against a thin screen of French outposts.

A tank battle broke out between Tirlemont and Huy on the morning of the 13th, following a typical onslaught by XVI Panzer Corps against the thin screen put out by the DLMs of the French Cavalry Corps. Stuka dive bombers flung their loads against the small knots of French Somuas mixed with light tanks, and the 3rd and 4th Panzer Divisions followed up with their customary vigour. Wherever tank met tank, the French failed to make capital of their slight superiority in armament, for this could avail them nothing once their isolated pockets had been bypassed and systematically attacked from front and rear by an enemy who always outnumbered them at the moment of action. By 1745 hours the French position had been infiltrated, withdrawal began – well ordered in places, hasty and panicky in others, but always beset by uncertainty and fears unchecked by tenuous control from above. The cavalry corps showed signs of premature disintegration as the XVI Panzer Corps forged ahead in an irresistible wave that began to funnel remorselessly along the important Perwez – Gembloux axis until stopped by the newly arrived French 1st Army on the line Wavre – Namur. According to the manuals, the DLMs had achieved the classic cavalry aim of shielding the occupation of the main defence position, and therefore there was no further immediate use for them, since, by the manuals, the mobile phase then gave way to positional warfare. The tanks of the DLMs could thus profitably be spread along the First Army front to add substance against an enemy who appeared to be committing his main armoured strength against Belgium – said the manuals.

What of the French tank crews? After two days' ignominious retreat before an omnipotent enemy, the standard operating procedures for them ceased to make sense. The losses they had inflicted in exchange for their own lacked significance in relation to their general sensation of having been worsted. From this moment the men of the DLMs lost confidence in their machines, their leaders, and themselves.

The XVI Panzer Corps had achieved a fine local success on the road to Gembloux – a success that established their superiority over the French mobile force but which, within the German Grand Design, represented no more than a diversion from the main effort aimed further south in the Ardennes. A further sharp attack by XVI Panzer Corps against French 1st Army made only slight headway and helped convince the French of German intentions against Belgium, but from that moment the Panzers gave up their attacks and suddenly withdrew. By then, in any case, all eyes had turned to dramatic events unfolding beyond Dinant.

Opposition by the French 9th Army amongst the forests of the Ardennes caused Rundstedt's Army Group 'A' less trouble than the traffic control problem involved in moving so many vehicles along the narrow twisting roads in time with a tight movement table. In three days all three Panzer Corps, the XV making for Dinant, the XLI for Monthermé and XIX for Sedan, each carrying supplies to make them self sufficient for nine days, and petrol for 100 to 125 miles, were overlooking the Meuse and preparing the main assault for the morning of 13th May. In XIX Corps the divisions had moved in line, followed by XLI Corps, making use of every road and track, few of which had been blocked in any way by an enemy who appeared utterly bewildered. General von Kleist, responsible for the whole of Army Group 'A's Panzer Group to Rundstedt, had disturbed Guderian at one moment by attempting to divert 10th Panzer from its original task to counter an unconfirmed threat by French cavalry, but

The sinews of victory. The tank in the foreground is a Czech 35t

apart from that Kleist had merely to await upon the results of a plan which had been accurately forecast at the War Games.

Long before the begininng of the offensive, Guderian had arranged for heavy close support by the Luftwaffe throughout the Meuse crossing. Guderian was to make the main attempt, while Reinhardt and Hoth widened the breach with only somewhat lesser forces – but with far less aerial support. Again Kleist intervened to superimpose a last minute plan of his own upon Guderian – altering Guderian's proposals (whereby the air attack would be one prolonged, dispersed bombardment, aimed at keeping the French gun positions quiet) to a more concentrated effort aimed at total destruction of the enemy positions in a short period.

It is the privilege of higher commanders to supervise their subordinates, and not unnatural that Kleist (who Guderian had reason to believe lacked confidence in the ability of the Panzer divisions) should exhibit anxiety just prior to the vital crossing of the formidable Meuse where it flowed between dominating heights. But last minute changes of plan can be fatal (on the old adage of 'Order, Counter-order, Disorder') – although in this case the revised orders to the Luftwaffe arrived too late for implementation. So the air plan stayed as originally conceived – to Guderian's immense relief. Mutual confidence between him and his superior had been shaken, however – an echo of the abiding disbelief in some quarters of the true potential of Panzer divisions.

All three Panzer corps launched their infantry across the river throughout the morning of the 13th. Along both banks the guns flashed, the Germans trying to subdue the enemy gun positions with their bombers and artillery, while their tanks shot up machine-gun nests on the far bank; the French laying protectives fire on

3-ton semi-tracked vehicle towing 10·5 cm. gun-Howitzer

the likely crossing places. All three Panzer corps were over by mid-afternoon – Guderian's with a strong infantry bridgehead that continued to expand while the engineers strove to construct a bridge to take the tanks: Reinhardt's hanging on with a toe hold at Monthermé, caught in a crossfire that successfully prevented progress and thoroughly hampered bridge building: Hoth's first across north of Dinant where the drive of Rommel's 7th Panzer Division carried it into the heart of a French tank counterattack.

By midnight only Reinhardt, alone of the three Panzer corps commanders, had failed to establish ferries or a bridge across the river, but both Hoth and Guderian were building up fast on the enemy bank, increasing their holding with every hour in a series of subtle infantry infiltrations amongst the disorganised French Ninth Army, and assembling together for the coming breakout. Yet the German threat was by no means overwhelming, and the French Ninth Army might well have contained the bridgeheads while destroying bridges from the air as they were constructed: they might easily

have wiped out Reinhardt's penetration. But General Corap, the commander of Ninth Army, had not emulated the practice of the German commanders of viewing the battle scene for himself. Accepting, at face value, the sort of pessimistic reports that nearly always emanate from a hard battle, he ordered a withdrawal on the night of the 14th – and opened the floodgates.

The Allied Air Forces might continue to attempt the destruction of the growing number of bridges over the Meuse, but by now the anti-aircraft defences were making this an unprofitable occupation. In any case, by the end of the 15th, the bulk of the German tanks were across with elements of 1st Panzer Division a good 15 miles to the east and 7th Panzer, under Rommel, 26 miles ahead, past Philipeville after a startling – and to conventional military minds – foolhardy lunge. For Rommel's spearhead – the 25th Panzer Regiment – could so easily have been isolated and destroyed. But Rommel sensed that the enemy were in no psychological condition to do so. They gave up in shoals, quite

often at the most tentative burst of machine-gun fire. From now on the Panzer divisions rolled forward almost at will, shooting up every conceivable sort of target on the way and gathering in hordes of prisoners who, in many cases, had absolutely no idea how the battle had reached them, many not having fired a shot.

Kleist's Panzer Group had achieved the aims of the War Games in six days. In the course of that time they had performed nearly every major operation of war with external assistance only from the Luftwaffe – encouraged to a certain extent by an opponent who had neither the skill nor the will to oppose effectively. A screen protecting a main position had been pushed in and, in parts, overrun. A strongly-held river line had been crossed in three places and the main positions behind eliminated. Local counterattacks had been rudely brushed off. Already there were signs that the Panzer divisions were beginning to dominate the minds of the French commanders – even, perhaps, to mesmerise them. Yet, on the night of the 15th, when the Panzers were on

the verge of confirming their ability to eliminate the Will as well as the Might of a whole nation, the men at the head of Germany's destiny began to falter and threaten to sacrifice the opportunities created for them.

Guderian had reached the critical moment when he must decide either to strike for Paris or for the English Channel via Amiens. His 1st and 3rd Panzer Divisions were advancing side by side, while Reinhardt started to make up for lost time on his right and Hoth strode ahead at the dynamic pace of Rommel's 7th Panzer Division. But on the evening of the 15th, Kleist, reflecting Rundstedt's and Hitler's anxiety that the infantry mass must line the flanks of the salient being driven into France, ordered a temporary halt. Arguing fiercely to be allowed to continue, Guderian managed to persuade Kleist to let him continue westward for another 24 hours – a concession of which he made full use by pushing on over 40 miles to reach Marle and Dercy, while Reinhardt almost caught up on entering Hirson. Again, however, Rommel stole the thunder by racing ahead with his

Panzer regiment to Clairfayts (constantly cursing the Rifle Regiments for falling behind in their soft-skinned vehicles) and there bumped into the somewhat rudimentary concrete pillboxes that represented the so-called Maginot Line Extension. Before nightfall the principal strongpoints had been reduced by a combination of Rommel's artillery and tank fire, followed by engineer demolitions rammed through the embrasures; soon work had started on breaking down the anti-tank obstacles and wire entanglements. All around burning French and Belgian houses lit up the scene – these sad night beacons etching the successive bounds reached by the Panzers across the full breadth of their swathe as the advance continued in the dark. Believing that unaimed suppressive fire could discourage enemy resistance, even though failing to cause heavy casualties, Rommel sent the entire Panzer regiment, guns blazing, in a mad rush between burning villages and broke clean through to Avesnes.

All through the night the advance went on, while the French Army stood foot-fast and surrendered in bewilderment. By 0730 hours on the 17th, Rommel had reached the outskirts of Le Cateau – his division strung out along a 50-mile corridor, with the gaps that had opened up between units filled by dumbfounded Frenchmen, some looking for ways to escape, others searching for surrender, and only a few engaging in combat. As flank guard to the main thrusts by Reinhardt and Guderian, his progress drew less attention from his superiors, But on the morning of the 17th. Guderian, whose 1st Panzer Division had reached the River Oise, was again told to halt – a peremptory order which drove him to fling his resignation at Kleist, who accepted it without hesitation. Rundstedt would have none of this and, through General List, told Guderian to continue to advance by subterfuge – that is, his Headquarters was to remain where it was while the rest of the corps carried out 'a reconnaissance in force'.

One element of the German High Command clearly recognised the possibilities opened up by the success of the Panzers matched to the failure

The spoils of victory – French tanks

of the French: another element, desperate to consolidate the gains with conventional forces, boggled at incurring further risks. The Germans worried continually lest the French should strike a properly organised blow at the ever lengthening flank of the corridor they were driving into the heart of France. But a blow such as that never came; the French reserves either melted away or were lost piecemeal in local counterattacks. Two unco-ordinated attacks such as this were mounted by the French 3rd and 4th DCRs – the latter commanded by Major-General Charles de Gaulle. The 3rd DCR attacked just south of Sedan, made an initial penetration, and was then taken in flank by 10th Panzer and rolled back: the 4th fought hard at Laon but was easily contained by 1st Panzer and forced into retreat despite the gallantry of the French crews.

After that the three leading Panzer corps had the field practically to themselves with the way to the Channel at Abbeville yawning wide open. To the north of the River Scarpe the British Expeditionary Force, along

with the Belgian Army and the French First, Seventh, and what remained of their Ninth Army stepped back eastwards and began to assemble a front protecting their terribly exposed southern flank. To the south the French armies which had escaped from Sedan tried to build up a new northern line protecting Paris. Of reserves to fling against the corridor there were next to none for the good reason that the best of them were already in dissolution, or half-trapped north of the Scarpe.

By 20th May, XIX, XLI and XV Panzer Corps, had reached a line stretching from Arleux on the River Sensée to Péronne on the Somme, and in rear followed XVI Panzer (released from its primary task in Belgium) threading its way through the slower moving infantry mass that was beginning to fill the gap between the Ardennes and the tip of the Panzer advance. By the night of 20th May, 2nd Panzer Division could see the English Channel from its new positions at Abbeville, 1st Panzer held Amiens, while 6th and 8th Panzer Divisions lay between Le Boisle and

Le Bassé. Rommel's 7th Panzer Division, after a series of adventures in which its commander repeatedly came close to personal disaster and his armour constantly got too far ahead of its infantry for comfort, lay close to the outskirts of Arras, with 5th Panzer left well behind on the other side of Cambrai. Now German tanks won victories where British tanks had shown the way in the previous war.

The Panzer exploitation from Sedan had been a headlong rush. Tactical flanking moves, such as there had been, were local and of limited scope. But now that the German army had inserted its main striking force deep within French territory and right across the Allied communications, an opportunity to achieve a major envelopment of the entire Allied army in Northern France and Belgium was presented. If the Panzers could turn swiftly from Abbeville and seize the ports from Boulogne to Dunkirk, the entire group of Franco-British armies would be cut off and forced to lay down their arms. Furthermore, on 21st May the Allies had no fighting forces near enough to the coast to stop the Panzers: their only hope of deflecting the Panzers could come from a counterblow against the flank and rear of the Panzer tip: but forces sufficient for such a profound blow could no longer be raised. Instead a small British probing attack with two heavy tank and two infantry battalions sallied forth against Rommel just as the latter was steering a short hook northwards towards Lille round the western environs of Arras.

Once again Rommel had sent 25th Panzer Regiment far ahead of the two rifle regiments, while the latter followed in their trucks, guarded by a screen of 37mm anti-tank guns. It was amongst these vulnerable infantry columns that 70 heavy British tanks discovered themselves as they advanced, and found that the thick British armour easily defeated the German anti-tank guns, so that the task of destroying the unprotected infantry could go on unhindered. Only after inflicting immense losses on the German infantry was the British attack halted in front of the rearward German field artillery positions and by a few 88mm anti-aircraft guns that happened to be deployed close to the front. Thus, for the first time, the '88' later to become famous as a tank killer, turned the scales in Rommel's favour. His own tanks played a most unprofitable part in the battle. Returning too late to save the unhappy infantry, 25th Panzer Regiment ran into a screen of British anti-tank guns and lost over 20 vehicles – while 5th Panzer Division, arriving in haste from Cambrai, merely mopped up the surviving British infantry.

From this inconclusive tank battle at Arras stemmed the chain of events which led to Hitler and the German High Command slowing down and finally halting the Panzer thrust to mop up the Channel Ports in rear of the Allied armies. The shock administered by an ill-planned but determined British local attack heaped one more fear onto a number of anxieties besetting the German generals. They anticipated another attack of greater dimensions from the same quarter, and realised it might cut off the whole Panzer force: they understood, too, that their declining tank strength caused by battle and mechanical losses, could soon deplete the force below the safety level, and jeopardise its chances of completing the conquest of the remainder of France: they thought that plunging the Panzer force into the waterways and built-up areas of Belgium might expose it to even heavier losses. So while the Allied armies retreated to Dunkirk, the Germans told their Panzer divisions to take Boulogne and Calais in a series of deliberate assaults, and pushed the weakened remnant of their forces only tentatively against the rapidly coalescing southern flank protecting the Allied retreat routes to Dunkirk.

By this time the Panzer divisions had gone through nearly the entire military repertoire, from 'advance to contact', through 'attack and breaching', to a full scale 'pursuit' interspersed with a fierce 'defensive tank battle'. Only a 'withdrawal' remained to be practiced – but that was some time off; there was never the need to try it during the French campaign. Only at Arras had the Panzers met really tough resistance of the sort that made them pause involuntarily. Here it was shown that the British possessed tanks that could out-gun the Germans and whose armour nullified the effect of German anti-tank guns. Here, too, Rommel learned that anti-tank guns acting in conjunction with armour were a formidable combination, particularly when that anti-tank gun was the 88mm anti-aircraft gun, especially when tanks could be lured (as had his own) onto a concealed anti-tank gun screen.

As far as the German High Command was concerned, the final elimination of the trapped Allied armies at Dunkirk could be left to the Luftwaffe, aided by supplementary land forces mostly provided by the infantry mass that pressed back the running British and French to the perimeter surrounding the port. Calais fell on 26th May releasing forces from XIX Panzer Corps to close in on Dunkirk from the south. But by then the port's defences bristled amongst inundations and any question of taking them with a rush had to be abandoned. On 28th May XIX Panzer Corps and the bulk of the other Panzer corps were withdrawn from the battle in order to rest and refit in preparation for their next task.

History tells us that the failure to destroy the British army at Dunkirk allowed the best of that army to escape and retrain for further battles. They were the first military organisation to evade the Panzers and be given the opportunity to study the lessons they had been taught in order to use them against their German tutors. Their 1st Armoured Division, meanwhile, was shipped to that part of France which had not been conquered to help the shaken remains of the French Army hold the line of the River Somme. The French had also learnt much and were in the process of establishing a deep defensive system amongst which they hoped to enmesh the next Panzer onrush. But the French army had lost its most powerful mechanised elements in Belgium – its survivors who escaped via Dunkirk by June 4th left all their equipment behind, and so could play no part in manning the chequer-board of strongpoints being built in villages and copses across the

The results of high mileage – a broken down Pz Kw IV

approaches to Paris. The open gaps between these strong-points, therefore, could only be covered by artillery fire unsupported by large concentrations of tanks. In short, the Germans had destroyed the best tools the French might employ for combatting tanks – French tanks.

German tank strength had been rapidly rebuilt to something approaching its initial level before the first German blow against metropolitan France fell on 5th June. A major re-grouping of the divisions had also taken place in order to construct five Panzer corps of roughly equal strength. The XV Panzer Corps, with 5th and 7th Panzer Divisions, was positioned close to the coast near Abbeville; XIV Panzer Corps, with 9th and 10th Panzer, lay close by Amiens along with XVI Panzer Corps with its 3rd and 4th Panzer Divisions – the latter Corps both in Panzer Group Kleist. North of Rethel a new Panzer Group under Guderian got ready to strike on 9th June using XXXIX and XLI Panzer Corps with, respectively, 1st and 2nd, and 6th and 8th Panzer Divisions.

General Hoth's XV Panzer Corps

began the offensive on the 5th with resounding success, making short work of the French attempting to screen the Somme crossing places, (which had been established the previous week) ferrying tanks across the rivers at a great rate (a mark of the excellent state of training that had been sharpened by live practice) and setting off on the kind of deep penetration that had won the first round of the campaign in Belgium. By 8th June both 5th and 7th Panzer Divisions were on the outskirts of Rouen, their flanks in process of being secured by the hard-marching infantry divisions that followed through the hole which had been torn in the French defences west of Amiens.

But Panzer Group Kleist was far from having its own way when trying to break out from bridgeheads at Amiens and Péronne, for here the French army rediscovered its old determination and fought back with desperate vigour. The new defence in depth proved quite hard to penetrate, for no sooner had the German tanks and infantry found what they thought to be a gap than it was to discover that they had, quite often, entered a trap – an artillery-fire killing ground. On those occasions when French tanks met the Germans in head-on conflict, the thicker armour of the French machines provided their crews with an important immunity that put the Germans at a temporary disadvantage. But overhead the Luftwaffe did much as it pleased, and bombed each French stronghold with impunity until, gradually, French resistance crumbled – Hoth's breakthrough to Rouen being the first important move and Guderian's attack with both his Panzer corps on either side of Rethel on 9th June, opening up a new front that posed a fatal threat to the rear of the still inviolate Maginot Line.

At first Guderian's Panzer Group met and was held up by resistance of the calibre which had stopped Kleist. Bridgeheads over the River Aisne were hard to take, French artillery fire hampered the engineers making tank crossing places, and counter-attacks kept the German infantry penned in. By the morning of the 10th, however, his tanks were across to the southern bank and from then on the rate of progress increased with ever greater speed. That same night Hoth's Corps, with Rommel's 7th Panzer Division in the lead, had reached the English Channel near St Valéry, cutting off the entire Allied army holding the coastal sector. And in the centre, Kleist's group, thwarted at Amiens and Péronne, had been switched rapidly eastwards to exploit Guderian's success and burst through, near Laon, to begin a parallel drive with Guderian's that thrust pincers round either side of Reims.

French military resistance now began to wither for lack of reserves. No longer could their defence in depth be given substance – but even had this been possible to the slightest degree it is unlikely that anything could have compensated for the utter collapse of their government and Higher Command's will to fight on. From the 10th onwards – if not before – the higher direction of the French war effort seemed to concentrate on seeking ways to mitigate the succession of blows and to finding a means to bring the war to an end.

Paris, the heart and mind of France, lay between two mighty Panzer pincers that threatened to close upon her any day. On 11th June, Panzer Group Kleist reached Chateau Thierry, crossed the River Marne, and continued to the south. Hoth's Corps threatened at any moment to emerge from the bridgeheads that had been taken over the Seine close to Rouen on the 9th. Thus Paris was threatened with total envelopment, while Panzer Group Guderian bypassed Reims on the 11th and began to exploit towards Chalons, beating off a last despairing lunge against its eastern flank by the sadly depleted French 3rd DLM and 3rd DCR out of the Argonne.

Paris no longer influenced the issue, for the French abandoned the city on the 13th, leaving the Germans to make a token entry with infantry next day. The vital battle was to be found where the Panzers led – straight into the industrial remnants of France and against the rear of the Maginot Line. The itinerary of each Panzer corps explained the magnitude of the collapse. Cherbourg fell to Rommel on 19th June – the beaten survivors of 1st British Armoured Division escap-

Breakthrough to the English Channel

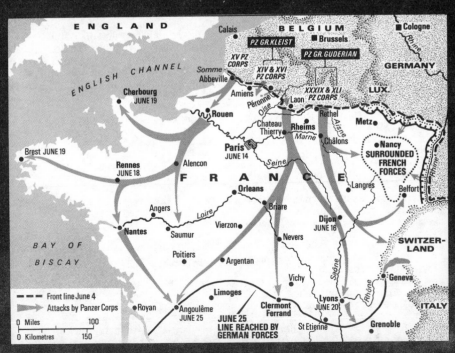

The final overrunning of France

ing as he arrived on the outskirts. Already Guderian had arrived on the Swiss frontier on the 16th, creating a vast, trapped pocket of French formations between his armoured flank and the fortified German frontier along the Rhine. On June 20th, Lyons fell just as the Italians – who had entered the war on the 10th – began an unhappy campaign endeavouring to emulate the Panzers in southern France.

But on 17th June Marshal Pétain, who had taken charge of the collapsing French government, told his people to stop fighting. He might have hung on longer and, indeed, there were many Frenchmen who prolonged resistance well past that date and some who fought on other fronts for the remainder of the war. Nevertheless, the means to perpetuate organised resistance had been destroyed. Initially this had been accomplished by the German armoured formations strongly backed by the Luftwaffe. Now, so broken were the French, even the conventional German infantry formations could advance with ease. For instance, General Manstein's 38th Infantry Corps covered over 300 miles from the River Somme to the River Loire in 13 days, fighting four major engagements on the way. But, without the disruption already inflicted on the French on both flanks by the Panzer corps, Manstein's feat would not have been possible.

On 25th June all fighting had come to an end in France. Rarely if ever before had a great nation such as this been subjugated with such speed and at such little cost to the attackers. German casualties from all causes amounted to a little over 156,000, the Panzer divisions' share being no more in proportion than that of other formations, even though they had seen most action and won the central victory. In material the losses amongst the Panzer divisions had been quite heavy – notably amongst the lighter tanks whose speed had not compensated for reduced armour protection. In gun power the Mark III and IV tanks had proved sufficient except when opposed by the handful of British Matildas and the French heavy machines. Thus, of a vast catalogue of technical improvements that

Above: Victorious leaders; *left:* von Runstedt, and *right:* Guderian. *Above right:* The triumphant elite. *Below right:* The failure of supply. A British Matilda set on fire by its crew

needed to be introduced, the desirability of increasing the gun power and armour protection of the tanks came first, for the British might appear again. But the need to give the rifle battalions in the Panzer divisions an armoured, cross-country vehicle which would enable them to follow the tanks more closely into action, seemed almost as important.

After June 1940, no German general worth his salt queried the decisive quality of the Panzer force. The French Campaign settled once and for all the basic uses to which its components could be put and established the principles of its handling. The fame of the Panzers was on everyone's lips – and nobody paid them greater praise than Hitler. To him, they represented the key to the subsequent conquest of the rest of Europe. Therefore his mind turned away from operations that looked unpromising for tanks towards schemes that seemed likely to suit the Panzer divisions. In this frame of mind he did all in his power to raise more Panzer divisions, sacrificing quality for quantity.

The triumphant élite

failure of supply –
British Matilda set on fire by its crew

49

Diversions
The southward urge

Bound for Yugoslavia

was many years before the rest of the world came to hear that Germany had conquered France with fewer tanks than the combined Franco-British forces had mustered. In July 1940 it was widely assumed that the catastrophic collapse of one of Europe's most vaunted military powers had been caused by a material inferiority in aircraft, tanks, and anti-tank guns, misguided by inadequate leadership. From then on only the British continued to stand in Hitler's way, and nobody expected her to last for long once Germany managed to transport Panzer divisions in an invasion fleet across the English Channel. Realising by now that Hitler's ambition knew no bounds, other nations turned to copy German military organisation, each calling for more aeroplanes, anti-tank guns, and, above all, more tanks. In the front line – in Britain – it was decided to form ten armoured divisions where not one existed complete (other than on paper) after the fall of France. In Russia the fatal practice of subjugating tanks to infantry formations was reversed to make way for the creation of tank and mechanised divisions with characteristics similar to those in Germany. And the Americans, who possessed neither many tanks nor a proper armoured force, feverishly adopted an armoured organisation (out of their Cavalry Branch), that in many ways aped the Germans, and applied her industry to making thousands of fighting vehicles in quantities the Germans could not hope to equal.

In Germany there was enthusiastic acceptance of the part the Panzers had played in France, and with it a desire to multiply the number of armoured formations. Unfortunately Hitler's demand for twice as many Panzer divisions as had fought in France could only be met by halving the tank strength of each existing division. Yet each new Panzer division required almost as much transport as the original organisation to keep it mobile, and this demand for extra motor vehicles, when added to another of Hitler's requirements for more motorised infantry divisions,

threw an unsupportable burden on the production resources of the German vehicle industry. To a certain extent the shortage of vehicles could be satisfied by drawing upon the vast haul captured from the West. French tanks could be adapted for use with Panzer divisions too, but their long-range performance did not match that of the German machines; and so a proliferation of different types raised problems in tactics, in training, and in the supply of spare parts.

In 1940 German production of new tanks of all types came to a little over 1,000 a year. In addition, a number of obsolete vehicles – mostly the original Mark Is, some Czech 38ts, and certain French types, were being converted to carry artillery or anti-tank guns. Guns of limited traverse when carried on a tracked chassis became known as 'Assault Guns' (manned by the Artillery, not the Panzer force), and were to be found chiefly in support of infantry divisions, while the basic tank, with its gun in a fully traversing turret, remained only with the Panzer divisions.

The shock administered by the British Matildas at Arras helped initiate a programme of upgunning the Mark III tank with a long 50mm gun, along with the up-armouring of both the Mark III and IV. But no great urgency was injected into designing radically more powerful tanks to succeed the existing types, although project studies on a new medium and a new heavy tank had been started, in 1937 and 1939 respectively. In the meantime, however, the production of armoured half-tracked infantry carriers went ahead apace in order to give the rifle regiments the capability of staying close to the tanks in action. But while the number of fighting vehicles with cross-country performance multiplied (by becoming increasingly track-borne) the supply columns remained road bound because they were comprised of wheeled vehicles.

A tremor of disquiet disturbed the victorious Germans when Britain did not give up in 1940, and when the Luftwaffe suffered defeat in the Battle of Britain – effectually stifling the plan to invade England. Unbeknown to all but his closest entourage, Hitler had already decided to attac Russia, confident that his army spearheaded by a larger Panzer force could crush the Russians in a singl brisk campaign. For this purpose th Wehrmacht reorganised throughou the winter of 1940/41, while Germa political and military influence wa extended throughout southern Europ and the Balkans – the essentia springboard for the southern pron of an invasion of the Ukraine.

Unfortunately for Hitler's plans however, his Italian partner, Mus solini, decided to win laurels for him self by invading Egypt's Wester Desert in September (only to b stopped by light mobile British force just inside the frontier), and b marching into Greece from Albania i November. In next to no time th Grecian venture degenerated into fiasco, the Italians finding themselve hard pressed to check the Gree counter offensive that rebounded int Albania. Then, in the first week o December, the British struck back i Egypt, wiped out a complete Italia army, and exploited so violently that by the first week in February, th whole of Cyrenaica and every majo Italian formation had been capturec At that moment it looked as if th small British armoured formation could advance almost unopposed t Tripolitania. This, as Hitler wel knew, would generate a politica crisis which his ally might not with stand.

The first of a number of mino diversions from the Russian ventur were thus forced upon Hitler. H agreed to prop up the Italian positio in North Africa with a fresh formatio called 'Afrika Korps' under the ma who had commanded 7th Panze Division with such vigour in France Erwin Rommel. Afrika Korps wa intended to consist of two divisons the first to sail, 5th Light Division landing its leading elements at Tripol on 14th February 1941. In fact, 5t Light was an early example of th forthcoming smaller Panzer division created by halving the tank compon ent of the original Panzer division and had only one Panzer regimen consisting of only two tank battalion with 90 tanks each, compared wit the old divisional complement of tw

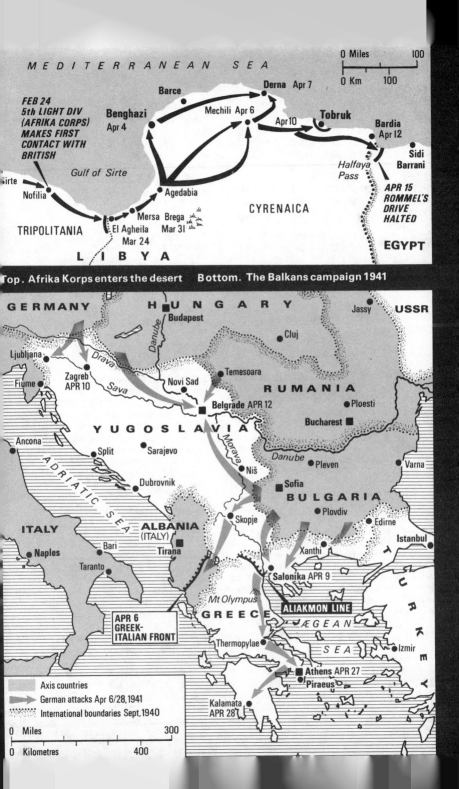

MEDITERRANEAN SEA

0 Miles 100
0 Km 100

**FEB 24
5th LIGHT DIV
(AFRIKA CORPS)
MAKES FIRST
CONTACT WITH
BRITISH**

Barce

Derna Apr 7

Benghazi
Apr 4

Mechili Apr 6

Tobruk

Apr 10

Bardia
Apr 12

Sidi
Barrani

Gulf of Sirte

Agedabia

*Halfaya
Pass*

irte

Nofilia

CYRENAICA

**APR 15
ROMMEL'S
DRIVE
HALTED**

TRIPOLITANIA

El Agheila
Mar 24

Mersa Brega
Mar 31

EGYPT

L I B Y A

Top. Afrika Korps enters the desert   Bottom. The Balkans campaign 1941

GERMANY

H U N G A R Y

Jassy

USSR

Danube

Budapest

Cluj

Ljubljana

Drava

Zagreb
APR 10

Sava

Novi Sad

Temesoara

R U M A N I A

Fiume

Belgrade APR 12

Ploesti

Bucharest

Ancona

Y U G O S L A V I A

Split

Sarajevo

Morava

Niš

Danube

Pleven

Varna

Dubrovnik

Sofia

B U L G A R I A

A D R I A T I C   S E A

**ALBANIA
(ITALY)**

Skopje

Plovdiv

Edirne

ITALY

Bari

Tirana

Istanbul

Naples

Xanthi

T U R K E Y

Taranto

Salonika APR 9

Mt Olympus

ALIAKMON LINE

**APR 6
GREEK-
ITALIAN FRONT**

G R E E C E

Æ G E A N

Thermopylae

S E A

Izmir

Athens APR 27
Piraeus

Kalamata
APR 28

Axis countries
German attacks Apr 6/28, 1941
International boundaries Sept, 1940

0 Miles 300
0 Kilometres 400

regiments of three battalions each. The 15th Panzer Division, which was intended to follow 5th Light to Africa, was originally meant to have three tank battalions in its Panzer regiment, but this too dropped to only two – in part a measure of the low priority granted to the African venture.

On February 24, Afrika Korps fought its first skirmish against the British in the desert, the overture to over two years' unbroken active service. They were very cautious, for the British were seasoned desert warriors whose victory over the Italians had demonstrated a keen comprehension of mobility. The Panzer soldiers knew they must learn to live and fight in a land that was devoid of all comfort and material aid. Everything they used, every drop of water they drank, and every gallon of petrol consumed by their vehicles, had to be carried to them. Moreover, temperatures that ranged from being bitterly cold at night to roastingly hot by day threw unaccountable strains upon the human body, while the clouds of dust eroded equipment in such a way that, for instance, tank engines wore out twice as quickly as in Europe.

In a land where cover could usually be found only amongst folds in the ground or in the uncharted spaces of the desert waste, tactics assumed a unique style. Battle could open at longer ranges, at which the judgement of distance became difficult and, often, distorted by heat shimmer. Tank gunnery took on a vital importance, and the supply of petrol and ammunition an all consuming preoccupation in the commander's mind. It says a lot for Rommel's leadership and the adaptability of the Panzer soldiers that they acquitted themselves with such devastating effect right from the start when, contrary to Hitler's wishes, they successfully attacked the British at Mersa Brega on 31st March.

Within 24 hours the British position, set in a narrow neck between the sea and some salt marshes, had been overrun, leaving a quantity of armoured vehicles and lorries in Rommel's hands. Seizing his opportunity, Rommel then raced eastwards in pursuit of an enemy who appeared as disorganised as had the French the previous May, confidently splitting his tiny force into three widel separated battle groups as he did s This was a procedure that had lon been recognised practice in the Panze divisions, but which had been use only to a limited extent in France du to the difficulty of keeping the infantr close to the tanks. Here in the deser infantry were perpetually vulnerabl in mobile conditions; there were fe places where they could fortify strongly dug in position – the onl sort of stronghold which could offe them security against tanks. S when the battle became mobile (as i usually did), the infantry had n option but to stay close to armour o anti-tank guns as part of an all-arm battle group. For them it became case of co-operate or perish.

By bluff and determination Romme outstripped the less mobile Britis forces whose worn out tanks, ham mered by the previous campaig against the Italians, and whose com manders (replacements for those wh had defeated the Italians) could no match Rommel's talent for oppor tunism. Within a few days the bulk o the British force, along with most o its leaders, had been netted betwee Benghazi and Mechili: the remainde took refuge either behind a ring o minefields and strongpoints in Tobru or with their backs to the Halfay Pass on the frontier of Egypt. Romme had demonstrated that, in mobil operations, constant motion is th secret of success and best insuranc against stalemate: simultaneously he learnt that exhausted men who hav run out of supplies as well as vitality are prone to error and doomed t failure when at the end of their tether

Met by a staunch, well-organise British and Australian mobile defenc that based its aggressive activitie upon the static Tobruk defences Afrika Korps came to a sudden stop The 5th Light Division had achieved a miracle in a fortnight; nevertheless it was the first Panzer division ever t be brought to an uncompromising halt.

Rommel failed in his first effort to break into Tobruk on 11th April – and failed in successive attempts again and again until 2nd May – even after the leading elements of 15th Panzer Division had arrived. In the meantime

eft. Heat
Right. Pz Kw IV in the sun and the dust

the situation on the other side of the Mediterranean had been transformed. The bloodless occupations of Rumania, Hungary, and Bulgaria looked, at one time, as if they might be succeeded by a similar pacifistic performance in Yugoslavia. After that the subjugation of Greece could be only a matter of time, for the latter's army was at full stretch holding the Italians in Albania, and, on Greek insistence, the British had refrained from sending an Expeditionary Force to help, in case it provoked German retaliation.

However, at the end of February, the Greeks drew the conclusion that German intervention in aid of Italy could no longer be delayed. Four British divisions were prepared in Egypt and joint Anglo-Greek planning put into effect, so that by the end of March nearly three of those divisions had arrived in Greece and were being deployed to guard Greece's frontier with Bulgaria and Yugoslavia. Then, suddenly, patriotic Yugoslavs rejected the prospect of 'peaceful' German occupation.

A challenge such as this could not be refused by Hitler. Not only was prestige at stake, but also the security of the southern flank of the vast invasion soon to be launched against Russia. Peaceful infiltration thus had to give place to violent aggression – its overture an indiscriminate aerial bombardment of Belgrade, the Yugoslav capital.

From the outset the Yugoslav position was hopeless. Her entire frontier, except that small part which was common with Greece, had been taken over by hostile elements. Her ill-equipped and poorly trained army was divided in its loyalties because of the traditional mistrust between Croats and Serbs that split the entire nation. The only factor in Yugoslavia's favour was her mountainous terrain. Therefore it was to be expected that the fighting would fall most heavily upon infantry divisions and mountain troops to the exclusion of Panzer divisions. Nevertheless, 9th Panzer Division's drive towards Skopje on 6th April, followed by 5th

Street battle – tank driver's view

Open warfare – tank gunner's target

Pz Kw II in a Grecian stream

57

and 11th Panzer Divisions towards Nis on the 8th, while 8th and 14th Panzer Divisions motored into northern Yugoslavia, making for Zagreb and Belgrade, unleashed a totally unexpected and, perhaps unwarranted, expenditure of effort in the German desire to achieve decisive results in the least possible time.

Events suggested that a hammer had struck the walnut, for the Croatian element of the Yugoslav army turned itself over to the Germans without a fight and the rest of the army crumbled, allowing the progress of the Panzer divisions along the difficult valley floors to resemble a peace-time exercise rather than a bloody operation of war. There was fighting in places, but none of significance; positions which might have been held indefinitely, amongst mountain peaks and close defiles, fell to the Germans at next to no cost. The operation enhanced the reputation of the Panzer divisions, gave them further practice in the art of movement and helped settle down the new organisations, but – unhappily for the future – it caused unwelcome wear and tear on equipment that would soon have to perform at maximum effort in Russia.

Greek resistance to the Germans was better organised, but barely more profitable than that of the Yugoslavs. In quick time the Greek defences protecting Salonika were breached from the east and turned by way of Yugoslavia from the direction of Skopje, thus letting the Germans loose throughout the whole of northern Greece and allowing them to descend upon the rear of the Greek army already engaged in Albania. By 16th April the entire northern front had collapsed as the Greek Army surrendered wholesale, leaving the British holding the line of the River Aliakmon almost in isolation. It had been hoped that the Greeks would stand in the mountains of central Greece, with troops who best knew that rugged territory, while the British covered the coastal plain with their more highly mechanised forces. The overthrow of the main Greek army put paid to this plan – and, indeed, left the British with no alternative other than to beat a rapid retreat

to the south.

The fact that they fought upon ground hallowed by the ancient feats of Athenians, Spartans, and Persians may well have crossed the minds of many of those in the German and British armies who grappled beneath the slopes of Mount Olympus and at Thermopylae. And like the Ancient Greeks when beset by the hosts of Persia, the British could only fight a rearguard, hoping to inflict as much damage as possible on the Germans in order to gain respite from a hot pursuit. The Germans, on the other hand, had no time to spare, and exploited the full versatility of their Panzer divisions. The 2nd Panzer Division, with its tanks blocked in impenetrable ground close to Olympus, dismounted its motor-cycle infantry and sent them on foot round the inland flank to disrupt the enemy position near the coast from the rear – a move that achieved complete success – while the tanks demonstrated to distract the attention of the British defenders.

Through excellent defensive country the British fell back, giving up many positions which, had

Pz Kw III in the Grecian mountains

stronger forces been available, might have been held indefinitely. At Thermopylae, where Leonidas once stood, the British stood too, and wreaked great execution with their field and anti-tank artillery. A whole company of 19 German tanks, trying to charge the pass, got jammed in its confines and was practically wiped out by close range fire. But this was a last defiant British gesture: enemy mountain divisions were bearing down on them from the mountains inland – and so the retreat to the sea had to continue. By the end of the month not one British soldier, other than the dead and prisoners, remained in Greece.

Once again the Panzer divisions had pulled off a mighty *coup*, their ingenuity in overcoming country totally unsuited to their characteristics leading the militarily uneducated (Hitler amongst them) to imagine that they might well be the ideal formation to tackle almost any kind of opposition. A cooler professional view might have noticed, however, that the almost total lack of a sound, armoured enemy had opened the way to the

Germans. There had been some British armour in Greece, but it was of an old, obsolete, and particularly unreliable type. Of 52 tanks in one regiment, only one was lost to enemy action: the rest broke down and had to be abandoned. So the Panzer divisions' 'magic' flowed from sources which, as yet, had not been fully explored.

Of all the Panzer generals, Rommel had most experience of fighting British tanks. He had been worsted by them at Arras in 1940 and taken revenge near Benghazi in April 1941. Rebuffed at Tobruk in May, he had first to consolidate the position at Halfaya on the Egyptian frontier before turning again to deal with Tobruk. A series of skirmishes presented him with a strong purchase on the Halfaya Pass, which he proceeded to fortify, using a few 88mm anti-aircraft guns to lay the foundation of the anti-tank defence. The lessons he had learnt at Arras were about to be employed to the further advantage of the Panzer divisions in defence. A defensive posture just had to be adopted since the arrival of 15th

Tank genius in the sun – Rommel in the desert

British Matildas – Nazi flag

running into difficulties against his anti-tank guns. But now it was the turn of Rommel's tanks to run into trouble against an unshaken enemy, who fought back hard – and the Germans were conclusively repulsed.

Once direct action had failed, Rommel whipped his Panzer regiments round the inland flank, aiming for the Egyptian frontier to cut off the British from their base, cascading the whole battlefield into a mad pattern of thrust and counter-thrust, and, eventually, bundling the British back whence they came.

In this battle the impact of evolving technology on tactics had been almost overriding. Neither side had demonstrated a marked technical superiority over the other, even though the British had introduced their new Crusader tank for the first time. The guns of medium tanks continued to penetrate each other's armour whenever they managed to score a hit – a remarkably infrequent occurence, as it happened. However, anti-tank guns – above all the 88s – dominated when lodged in safe defensive positions, and, since none of the British tanks could fire high-explosive shells and their artillery did not often work closely with the tanks, this domination was hardly challenged. Even the heavy British Matildas had fallen victim to the 88s, but when German tank guns hit the Matildas in individual combat, the thick armour of the British machines defeated the shot and baffled the German crews at a time when tank versus tank actions were becoming more common. Tactics could be devised to mitigate technical deficiencies, but the confidence of the crews suffered if they were asked to contrive too much in the heat of action. There is a limit to the subtlety of a frightened man. Clearly the German tanks needed a more powerful gun that could penetrate the best enemy armour at longer ranges than they themselves could be penetrated by the enemy.

Panzer Division to join 5th Light had worsened the shortage of supplies that precluded any prospect of offensive operations for the time being. In any case, as June passed, it became clear that the British themselves were about to attack.

Tanks are an offensive weapon to be used when the enemy is off balance in order to achieve their maximum effect. In defence, Rommel raised a crust of localities behind the Egyptian frontier, placing infantry units under the protection of anti-tank guns, but holding the Panzer regiments deep in the rear from whence they could either strike south to the frontier or east against Tobruk should the garrison try to join in the British offensive. This represented the classic use of armour in defence.

When the British made a direct attack on Halfaya Pass and swung fast cruiser tanks round the desert flank on 15th June, the German 88mm guns completely smashed the attack at Halfaya, and blunted the inland hook. Thereupon Rommel committed his own armour, in an effort to catch the British tanks just as they were

Russia
The strain
of disillusionment

Into the void – Guderian watches his Panzers advance into Russia

A German Panzer officer has described the summer of 1940 as the happiest of the war. The Wehrmacht basked in contentment at its achievements, for it seemed that soon the war would be over, since the British could hardly be expected to hold out for long against insuperable odds. Thus, only Russia offered a significant military presence in Europe, but she was bound to Germany by the pact of August 1939 (which had triggered off the invasion of Poland), and Russia was a vast enigma, known to have equipped her enormous army with a great tank fleet comprising many up-to-date machines. To attack her might invite disaster; yet, on 21st July, 1940, Hitler decided to do that very thing in the following year.

The German dictator had come to power on the back of an anti-Communist political campaign, so nobody could reasonably expect him long to remain a contented ally of the nation which promoted the Communist doctrine throughout the world. He knew – and so did the Russians – that the day must dawn when the two countries

would collide. Reasoning that, with France out of the way, Britain enfeebled, and the Luftwaffe and Panzer force approaching the peak of professional perfection, Hitler believed that the crowning mercy of his plan to dominate Europe need no longer be delayed. Moreover, he persuaded himself that the image of immense Russian strength was a false one, appreciating, with some reason, that a series of violent political purges had deprived the Russian officer corps of the best of its most incisive and independent brains, and seriously weakened the *esprit de corps* of their whole army.

In material and manpower the Russians enjoyed a ponderous superiority over the Germans. They had something like 20,000 tanks, of which over a thousand were the excellent T-34 (with its well-shaped armour providing fine protection), and the heavier KV-1 – both armed with a good high velocity 76mm gun, and technically well in advance of any German tank in service. But the majority of Russian tanks were of

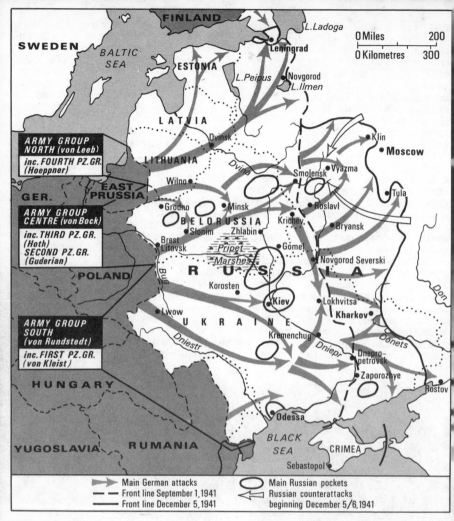

The drive in Russia 1941

Map legend:
- Main German attacks
- Front line September 1, 1941
- Front line December 5, 1941
- Main Russian pockets
- Russian counterattacks beginning December 5/6, 1941

lesser calibre, many dating from the earliest days of Russian tank production, some light machines based on original British Vickers designs, others the forerunners of T-34 – the fast cruisers, BT-2, 3, 5 and 7 which drew their origins from the designs of the American, J Walter Christie. There were also some very heavy tanks of ponderous size. Russian fighting vehicles were either armed with a 37mm, a 45mm, or a 76mm gun, but in June 1941 nearly 60% of the older ones were out of action for mechanical reasons – a disquieting insight into the

unreliability of the machinery and the ineptitude of the crews. Meanwhile, the brand new T-34s and KV-1s were in course of being incorporated into new tank and mechanised divisions – Russia's response to the German Panzer divisions – and so the crews were far from being accustomed to their new equipment or the role they were meant to play.

Hitler, as we have seen, had doubled the number of his Panzer divisions, but not the total German tank strength. In June 1941, 3,200 tanks could be mustered against Russia –

only a few more than had been used in France, although, of course, there were a great many additional Mark IIIs and IVs (the 37mm gun had almost disappeared from tank service) substituted for the obsolete light tanks. Some 20 Panzer divisions were available – all, except six of them, having only two tank battalions each; the other six with three battalions each. Panzer divisions continued to be commanded by Panzer corps (usually one or two per corps, grouped with a motorised division and, sometimes, an infantry division), and two of these Panzer corps were usually to be found in Panzer groups within the field armies – an indication that the Germans could not permit the Panzer hierarchy to seize operational control for themselves. But since the quantity of tanks remained almost constant while the number of units increased, the only real increase, since 1940, rose from a multiplication of the number of controlling headquarters. This could enhance the flexibility of command – but it could also introduce the kind of creeping paralysis that infests bureaucracy – the sort of decadence defined by Professor Parkinson.

Hitler fought his battles from maps using coloured symbols that meant more to him than the flesh, blood, and tanks that those symbols represented. He was a politician who sensed – not an educated soldier who calculated and who knew that, in the last analysis, it is the man, not the machine, who wins battles. So political motives overrode military considerations during the planning of the invasion of Russia. Hence the fluctuations in an evolving strategy waxed as virulent in the winter of 1940/41 as they had a year earlier before the invasion of France. Nevertheless professional preferences dictated variations on every scheme emanating from the councils of war, and overall there hung a sickly apprehension since, from the outset, hardly a single German in the know could dismiss from his mind the awful spectre of Napoleon's fate a hundred years back.

By degrees the final plan (Operation Barbarossa) came into being. In outline it demanded that the southerly sector of the Southern Front should be watched by the Rumanian and Hungarian Armies while, from its northerly sector, Field-Marshal von Rundstedt's Army Group South struck powerfully (led by Kleist's Panzer Group) towards Kiev. Meanwhile Field-Marshal von Bock's Army Group Centre was to launch the main blow towards Moscow via Minsk and Smolensk, employing the two strongest Panzer Groups (Guderian's and Hoth's), while Field-Marshal von Leeb's Army Group North (with Hoeppner's Panzer Group) advanced to take Leningrad. The plan etches Hitler's political aims – the objectives were communication and ideological centres; only second priority was given to the capture of industrial zones and the highly important work of destroying the Russian field armies seems to have been taken for granted within the main political framework.

To the German military hierarchy the one and only worthwhile goal was the destruction of the Russian army, and their chief agent in attaining it the Panzer groups. Unhappily, the German generals could not agree amongst themselves how best to control the Panzer groups. The keenest amongst the Panzer protagonists – generals such as Guderian and Manstein - wanted to cut loose with the Panzer groups and roam at large, deep in the wide open spaces that could be found in the Russian rear once the initial breakthrough had been made: the infantry formations, they said, should follow up as quickly as possible in order to surround and annihilate a bewildered enemy. The more orthodox commanders accepted that the Panzer groups represented the striking force of each army or army group, but insisted that they should work in conjunction with the main body in completing the annihilation of trapped forces. Both schools of thought appreciated that Panzer divisions on their own could not for long hold the rings cast round strong enemy bodies – but the deep raiding school dreamed mainly in terms of disruption (holding that, in any case, the safety of the Panzer divisions depended upon their constant movement keeping the enemy in perpetual doubt), while the conventional school considered that, if the Panzers got separated too far from the main body,

both might be defeated before they could come to each other's help. The argument was not really resolved before the start: Panzer groups remained under army control – in theory – but in practice the Panzer group leaders thought and acted on their own terms.

Rarely before has such a military concentration taken place as that which gathered west of the Russian frontiers from the Arctic Circle to the Black Sea throughout May and June 1941. Movement went on mostly by night, taking the utmost care to conceal the enormous concourse of men and machines and the vast dumps of supplies hidden in towns and forests. Amongst the last to arrive – because their presence alone foretold an offensive – were the Panzer divisions – some coming straight from Central Germany where they had been engaged in intensive training, but those belonging to Kleist's group post haste from the invasion of the Balkans. The latter, particularly the elements which had reached the south of Greece, had serious need of servicing after running hundreds of miles: the Balkan campaign had taken its toll.

The men were in fine fettle, fully confident in their battle-craft, their equipment, their leaders and their cause. But the coming task was daunting, for a dweller from Central Europe has an acute sense of history and instinctively dreads the emptiness of the Russian spaces. Of course the whole operation fermented in deepest secrecy for as long as possible, even some of the more senior commanders being unaware of its target: for instance Manstein did not know until May.

The Russians could not be entirely hoodwinked by German protestations of non-aggression and life-long friendship. For weeks they had been aware of the threat building up to the west and for months they had laid out strengthened defences to stop the attack if and when it came; indeed, their dispositions were entirely defensive, lying passively in great depth well behind the frontier. Little or no positive warning came to activate their forward elements, the first notice many received of the German onslaught being the fall of bombs and the arrival of tanks in their midst – a surprise made more complete by the Germans using deep wading tanks, with only a breathing tube showing above the surface, to cross the bed of the River Bug.

Rapidly the arrows of Hitler's battle maps spread out across Russian territory. But to those actually trying to read the ground from the smaller scale maps, serious discrepancies lead to unhappy confusion; quite often the maps did not resemble the country they depicted; above all the main motorway said to lead to Moscow was nowhere completed, and these discrepancies upset almost every plan, slowed operations, and made it difficult to direct supplies to the right place, while repeatedly it became impossible to drive along the tracks that served for roads. Frequently the tanks' tracks destroyed the very life lines upon which their supplies ought to have moved. However, by 24th June, Army Group Centre had effected its first encirclement of major Russian forces near Slonin, where Guderian's Panzer Group curled up from Brest Litovsk and the 9th Infantry Army marched down from Grodno. Meanwhile Hoth's Panzer Group reached Wilno and kept going in fine style towards Minsk, leaping ahead as Guderian's group broke eastwards from Slonin to begin another even greater encirclement that closed its jaws to the east of Minsk on 29th June when it met Hoth's group.

On the map the Panzer arms looked perilously slim, as indeed they were; and those thin tentacles were severely and repeatedly tested when Russian counterattacks began in earnest on the 24th. At first only local and desultory probes had to be brushed off, but as time passed these probes became full-scale assaults, pressed home with fanatical determination, but lacking in overall co-ordination. A flurry of tank versus tank engagements blazed up, and in the extremely confused situations which arose, when both sides became entangled, the superior German systems of command and control helped them to take charge, while the older Russian tanks succumbed to the more modern German weapons. Much the same could be reported from all fronts: where the ground was dry and firm, the tank attacks moved without pause and the supply lorries followed easily to help keep up momentum.

The truly remarkable advance by Manstein's Panzer Group in Army Group North to Dvinsk (Dangavpils), 200 miles in four days, demonstrated the sort of independent action produced by that outstanding German Commander. At one time his 8th Panzer and 3rd Motorised Divisions were over 50 miles ahead of the rest of the Group, having bypassed three Russian corps. Here the Russians reacted in confusion, some bent on withdrawing to Dvinsk, while others tried to cut the narrow corridor through which the rest of the Fourth Panzer Army, under Hoepner, were trying to squeeze in order to join Manstein. Cheerfully composed, Manstein felt comparatively safe in the belief that his sweeping advance had completely unsettled the enemy. His main anxiety was to be told where to go next, for he abhorred holding a crossing over the River Dvina (for the use of the slower Sixteenth Army) thus giving the enemy every chance to concentrate against him.

But Manstein had far outstripped Reinhardt's Panzer Corps on his left – a delay caused in part by Russian technical superiority. Two battlegroups of 6th Panzer Division in Reinhardt's Corps had broken through on 23rd June, but later it was discovered that a Russian KV-1 sat astride the main supply route. Efforts to send wheeled supply vehicles cross-country stuck in the forests and nearby swamp; attempts to shoot the KV with 50mm anti-tank guns from 1,000 yards failed to penetrate the Russian armour, and the KV coolly picked off 12 50mm guns in turn with its 76mm gun – similar target practice being repeated upon an 88mm anti-tank gun before it could be set up for action. Just 24 hours later the KV was still there – quite unmoving – until an 88 was manoeuvred behind it and put two shots through the rear of its turret.

The sheer dogged persistence and immovability of the Russian soldiers were the most terrifying things about

The endless Steppe

them. The Germans manoeuvred and cut them off by the thousands – till they waited for more. Nearly 30 Russian divisions were encircled by Army Group Centre's pincer at Minsk, and vast quantities of material netted; but a great many Russian soldiers managed to slip away where the Panzer cordons were not thick or deep enough to seal all the escape routes. No tactical liberties such as had been taken in France could be taken in Russia, as 3rd Panzer Division discovered on 6th July, when, advancing as part of Army Group Centre's southern flank guard during the attempt to trap yet another block of Russian armies near Smolensk. Closing upon Zhlobin without bothering to take their infantry with them, or putting out adequate scouts, 40 German tanks passed an enemy artillery position quite unobserved, and then came under close-range fire from 30 Russian tanks hidden in buildings on the outskirts of the town. Swinging away, they then took further losses when concealed Russian artillery opened fire from the flank. Some 22 tanks were lost and the situation redeemed only because another battalion of German tanks entered Zhlobin unobserved at the height of the initial action, and destroyed nearly every Russian defender from the rear without loss to themselves.

South of the Pripet Marshes, Kleist's Panzer group in Rundstedt's Army Group South met and broke one Russian force after another when they attempted to deny or hold successive lines of defence – rather like the French the year before. Eliminated on open ground, those of the enemy who evaded capture retired into the marshes or into great townships such as Kiev, both of which were more or less out of bounds to Panzer divisions which lacked both the strength and the facilities to prevail there.

Amongst the military virtues best practised by the Germans in all their earlier campaigns, was the discipline of minimising casualties: where opposition was likely to be heavy they were reluctant to follow – the more so as they increasingly realised that Russian resistance might be a force beyond their strength. Rundstedt would not permit Panzer divisions to charge into Kiev or into the Pripet Marshes. Instead he kept his mechanised forces moving freely in the plains where they dominated, and was content to complete a gigantic encirclement of the best part of two Russian armies east of the River Bug by 8th August.

The campaign was six weeks old, the longest ever undertaken by a mechanised army, and the machines were beginning to show signs of severe wear and tear. After every previous campaign tanks had been withdrawn to Germany where a central servicing organisation refurbished them. This was a routine procedure, and so no decentralised servicing system had been provided for use in the field since the necessity was not expected to arise. Now that it had, the spares (and the technicians to use them) remained in Germany, while tanks broke down in Russia. Furthermore, battle losses were the highest ever experienced against an enemy who fought with the same tenacity as the British; the Wehrmacht in Russia simply learned what Afrika Korps had already suffered on a much smaller scale in the desert. And like Afrika Korps at Tobruk, the Wehrmacht stalled in its tracks. Guderian and the other Panzer leaders implored Hitler to send them new tanks, new engines, and reinforcements. Each general still thought mainly of his own front, imagining a triple advance could be maintained, as in June, when, in point of fact, Hitler had no option but pick each new offensive in strict priority to the next.

The first week of August stilled the initial onrush of the German invasion. It had been hoped that, by then, decisive results would have been achieved bringing the Russian armies into dissolution. This was far from the case. Army Group North was actually encountering stiffer resistance than ever close to Lake Ilmen, in the approaches to Leningrad, and only reached Novgorod on the 16th. After completing another annihilating round-up of Russian forces in the Smolensk area by mid-July, and crossing the River Desna at the end of the month, Army Group Centre thought it saw the way to Moscow wide open. It had come 400 miles – another 200 was well within its scope, so it said. But the German High Command was neither committed to a drive on Moscow, nor ready to give a decision to strike further east until Army Group South's territory had been cleared up.

Fairly strong Russian forces still blocked the direct approach to Moscow, as Guderian's Panzer Group found between Roslavl and Smolensk on 3rd August when their local offensive provoked an avalanche of poorly co-ordinated Russian counterattacks. Between Gomel and Kiev even bigger Russian Armies – the 5th, 21st, 26th, and 37th – lay almost moribund, having been pushed there by Army Group Centre and Army Group South. This Russian concentration posed a serious threat to the southern flank of Army Group Centre and, by Hitler's order, was next to be destroyed while at the same time further assistance was to be given to Army Group North: thus the drive to Moscow had to wait while the front was tidied up.

Indeed, everything had now to wait for supplies, for Russia could provide very little to sustain a petrol-driven army of the size of the Wehrmacht – there were no residual petrol storage depots, the roads and tracks could not carry for long the sort of heavy traffic needed to transport the large stocks essential to a further advance. The railways had been efficiently demolished, bridges were down and, in any case, rail track gauge had to be converted to the German standard. Not until the last week in August could sufficiently large stocks of essential supplies be accumulated to supply the two great Panzer-tipped spearheads as they set off – Guderian's southward from Krichev past Novgorod Severski, and Kleist's northward over the Dneipr close by Kremenchug.

At the start, nearly 400 miles separated these two prongs, while to the east the Russians desperately gathered fresh forces with which to hack at the flank of Guderian's advance. Inside the pocket which the Germans planned to encompass, 650,000 Russian soldiers were fighting – those in 21st Army actually partaking

Close support for the Panzers – Stuka dive bombers

in an offensive between Novgorod Severski and Gomel. Within an arena of such enormous dimensions, the Panzer divisions and their infantry associates occupied hardly any space at all – in a way they were lost. The gaps between formations became ever wider – on one occasion an infantry division policed (it could never hold) a front some 60 miles wide – but where the belligerents bumped into each other – usually close to or about some nodal point – formations closed up and their units fought at the sort of density for which they were designed. Since neither side (and least of all the Germans) had forces sufficient to cover the vast areas of Russian space, they had to rely more and more on rapid mobility to fill wide gaps. Thus the Panzer divisions held sway, appearing and disappearing, fighting between one refuge and another, hunting the enemy and being hunted themselves, and using the increased range of their weapons to compensate for the deficiencies in numbers.

When the German pincers eventually closed the northern and southern points of their Ukrainian encirclement at Lokhvitsa on September 15, they left in their wake a trail of destruction, gathered to their cages a mounting flood of prisoners (many of whom surrendered most willingly), and garnered unbelievable riches in warlike material as they closed round the edges of the vast pocket centred on Kiev. But any Russian with the wit and determination to escape the narrow Panzer cordon could do so – as many did, escaping either to the east or into the western forests and swamps to join Partisan guerilla bands, where tanks could not follow them and where any man with rifle in hand was the equal of a German infantryman deprived of armoured assistance.

Yet another Panzer victory accrued to Hitler's credit – and still the Russians fought on, while Leningrad endured a state of siege from the end of August onwards, behind lines that could not be penetrated. Germans who had pleaded to be allowed to drive to Moscow in August now faced the possibility of having to do so in October – but already the first of Mother Russia's natural allies – mud – had come to her assistance.

Shortly would follow its inveterate successor, the deep winter freeze, to solidify the quagmires but introduce yet more formidable difficulties to bar the way to further exploitation of the German campaign; and logic told the soldiers – and Hitler too if he had cared to listen – that the campaigning year in Russia had passed. Complete victory had eluded the German grasp, but the line upon which Hitler's armies stood at the end of September offered a sound defensive base from which the offensive might be renewed in 1942. The Russians might regather their strength in the meantime, but at least the German army, whose losses to date had been trifling, could winter in security within reach of supplies that could be fetched with relative ease from their homeland. In circumstances such as these any Russian winter counteroffensive that might be launched, should be contained.

But Hitler's ego would not let him stop, and the brilliant success of the Panzer divisions warped his faulty judgement. He projected not one but two new thrusts – the first, starting on 30th September, aimed at Kharkov, the industrial lower Don and the oil-bearing Caucasus: the second on 2nd October, a massive triple drive by the three Panzer groups of Army Group Centre to seize Moscow. Meanwhile, Army Group North tightened its grip on Leningrad, knowing that it could not penetrate the suburbs and thereby forecasting the slim chances of Army Group Centre should it reach Moscow.

For the next three weeks the course of events pursued an almost stereotyped pattern. Both new major offen-

Counter-attack – an anti-tank gun crew on the alert

The liberators and Russian peasants

50mm Anti-tank gun Pak 38
Introduced in 1941 to replace the 37mm gun, this model became the foundation of German anti-tank defence when it worked alongside the more powerful 88mm dual purpose gun. In the Panzer Division it would provide the pivot for manoeuvre as flank defence. Using AP 40 shot it attained a muzzle velocity of 3,940 feet per second which meant that it could penetrate 56mm of armour sloped at 30° at 1,000 yards range

sives broke through, plunged deep into the enemy rear, surrounded pockets of Russian formations, closed on them, captured those that could not break out, and then hunted eastwards seeking further prey. So heavy had been the earlier Russian casualties – particularly in tanks – that they were actually outnumbered on most local fronts for the first time. The road to Moscow lay wide open and the Panzer groups, had they not been committed to reducing Russian pockets, might have driven there without much bother. But the sacrifice of the Russian masses in the pockets gave the Soviet High Command valuable time in which to improvise supplementary defences closer to their capital. The same kind of mute resistance held up Army Group South after they had penned a sizeable Russian army east of Zaporozhye. So, when both principal Army Groups were ready to set off again in mid-October having consummated their pyrrhic victory, it was only to repeat the old formula, but this time in an altogether stiffer manner.

The Russians were evading the pincers with greater skill, and since they were being pressed back against a secure base, were gaining strength as they went, while the Germans dissipated their numbers along lengthening and crumbling frozen roads and tracks. And whenever it thawed, as often it did, the mud liquified and then glued all further movement be it on roads or cross-country. In conditions such as these, the wide steel tracks on the Russian armoured vehicles gave them a significant advantage over their German opponents, for the latters' tanks ran on narrower tracks with a higher track-to-ground pressure that allowed them to sink into mud or snow much sooner than the Russian tanks. This fundamental technical superiority had much to do with the better performance of the Russians in the earlier stages of winter warfare: simply put, until the Germans had acquired broad tracks of their own, the Russians could often move when the Germans stuck fast.

Nevertheless, it said volumes for the ingenuity of the Germans, and the feeble state to which the Russians had been reduced, that the advance continued. Progressively the German soldiers suffered greater agonies in the freezing cold and the winter snows; the mean temperature in January 1942 fell as low as —32° F on the Moscow front.

As Moscow got closer, the German generals took to reading Caulaincourt's harrowing account of Napoleon's 1812 campaign. But Napoleon had mainly to deal with flesh and blood; the Germans in 1941 had also to cope with the infinite complexities of mechanisation when the mechanical state of their army – above all its tanks – sank in decline.

Deciding that centralised servicing in Germany had to give way to a decentralised system in Russia, the Germans tried to ship great loads of spares to the front. Unfortunately the staffs were unfamiliar with a problem that had, until recently, been an industrial responsibility, so spares went adrift. For instance, Army Group South received several loads of spares for tank models it did not possess, when Army Group North was in dire need of those very parts. The countryside became littered with irreparable tanks which could not be shifted back to the Fatherland for Base Repair, down clogged routes, which could barely support the forward transit of spares to repair tanks in location. The mainspring of the Panzer armies was thus running down – and with it the offensive power of the Wehrmacht.

It came as a surprise to Hitler when all forward movement ground to a halt at the end of October: he just had not grasped the delapidated state of his forces or the resilience of the desperate Russian resistance within the depths of the mother country. If an offensive at the end of September had looked like a gamble, its resumption in an effort to encircle Moscow at the end of November was tantamount to military suicide. Tank strengths were desperately low, the men's fighting spirit curdled by the cold, vehicles freezing up with cracked cylinder blocks – the whole army creaking and groaning because no preparations had been made for a winter campaign.

Yet a last effort to break into the Russian capital was made – Field-Marshal von Kluge going in person to the front line to consult with the junior officers as to its feasibility – but the majority of commanders could resort only to emotional exhortations to achieve the necessary enthusiasm. This time, however, only the barest progress was made, for the men were beset by a myriad harassing counterattacks from all directions at frequent intervals, and had in any case to spend almost as much time striving to keep alive in the freezing blizzards as in actual combat.

From amongst the forests close to Moscow, 2nd Panzer Division saw a fleeting glimpse of the Kremlin in the distance and a few infantrymen broke into the suburbs, only to be expelled by workers debouching to defend their factories. On 5th December all further German offensive operations had to stop, for that day the Russians launched their first major winter counter offensive.

Already Rundstedt's arrival on the River Don at Rostov had been the signal for a successful counterattack by the Russian 37th Army. The Germans took Rostov on 21st November, but were ejected on the 30th and forced to fall back with the Russians in pursuit. For the first time, Panzer divisions fought in full retreat, holding off the enemy in order to give the rest of the army time to escape, and thereby reversing the familiar attack procedure when they used to open the way to make room for the rest of the army to advance; in other words, Panzer divisions could close doors as well as open them. Army Group South managed to retain a grip on the situation and had need to come back only a few score miles, but on the Moscow front the situation was far more desperate. There the Russians took a leaf from the German book, and sought to envelop Army Group Centre in the grand manner by thrusting out the horns of a double offensive from either flank in the direction of Vyazma.

Caught in a dreadful predicament, the Germans could only retreat although Hitler's 'stand and fight' order did much to stiffen resistance and prevent the panic that might easily have set in. Without studied preparation, the German army had now to teach itself the art of with-

And the first Russian tank crews surrender

drawal after two years' perpetual advance. Even so, well-versed tactical tenets remained sacrosanct – to stay concentrated in moments of crisis along with the need to find security on one base or line after another when in motion.

A grim determination to leave as little as possible to the enemy instinctively permeated German conduct. The wounded had to be evacuated if possible: tanks must also be recovered, for both were precious and the latter, if not recovered, must be rendered useless.

The action by 1st Panzer Division at Klin recorded a fine example of a typical withdrawal, and also describes an early German venture in escape from encirclement. When Hoepner's Panzer Group began to withdraw from the northern outskirts of Moscow, it sent back 1st Panzer to hold open the road at Klin through which the rest of the group and Fourth Army could escape to the west. After severe fighting in an almost static role – a role quite unsuited to a mobile formation – the task was accomplished; but at the expense of 1st Panzer Division finding that it had itself been cut off. In order to ease the breakout past strong enemy blocking positions barring the most obvious route, a rifle company was sent to stage a diversionary attack to draw the enemy away from the principal blocking positions – an order made that much more effective in that the riflemen were not told that theirs was a sacrificial effort. The 1st Panzer Division had been temporarily surrounded once before during their original advance: now they merely repeated tried tactics in reverse – and with success, for the Russians rose to the bait, left their main positions to beat off the diversion, and let the whole mobile body of 1st Panzer escape, full tilt, down the road. Every tank, truck, and tractor that would run raced along, while the artillery bombarded the enemy until its turn to go had come. The wounded travelled under escort, only a few prisoners were lost, and abandoned equipment was blown up or burnt. Twenty-four hours later the division was again in action on another part of the front.

Often in desperate straits, but rarely in collapse, the retreating Germans fought off wave after wave of fresh but amateurish Russian divisions. To the incredulous Germans it seemed as if all their victories had multiplied rather than diminished the enemy. Indeed an assessment of the enemy's strength issued by the German High Command in December 1941 put the Russians at no less than 200 infantry and 35 cavalry divisions, along with 45 tank brigades – all on the main front – while many more formations were to be found elsewhere in that gigantic country. In fact this gave the Russians twice the German numerical strength – though in training and all round ability the scales still fell well upon the German side. The wide frontages of these Russian offensives only indicated overwhelming numbers, not skill, since they came into action in the most unsophisticated manner, winning their gains by sheer numbers, and suffering appalling casualties in the process. True, whatever losses the Germans suffered were qualitatively serious, for they represented the cream of a brilliant army; but even the Russians had to improve quality one day and could not afford interminable massacres.

Once the initial panic had subsided and the novelty of being in retreat worn off, the Germans reverted to their customary skilful conduct of operations. Seeking shelter from the cold as much as from the enemy, they established defensive 'hedgehogs' in the towns and villages, mostly where routes converged. Around these the Russian attacks would ebb and flow while supplies were flown in by the Luftwaffe, or fought through by mobile forces. A great deal of ground had to be given up and much material (quite a lot of it Russian) disgorged in the process, while the Panzer divisions acted as fire brigades called to control each Russian outbreak once it appeared to be getting out of hand. Repeated German counterattacks nearly always baffled the Russians, who had yet to learn how to cater for the unexpected: surprise was the very essence of Panzer division warfare, be it in attack or in defence.

But counterattacks demanded

mobility – and this foundered in wildly changing temperatures, when one moment vehicles would be bogged in mud and the next moment frozen fast by a sudden cold snap. Caught in the open by a succession of temperature fluctuations just at the moment when they were being harried by the Russians, 6th Panzer Division lost all its vehicles and was reduced for a while to little above company strength: indeed, for some weeks this division fought on foot simply because it had lost every single prime mover.

But by the end of March the front had been stabilised, with the Russians exhausted and the Germans resurgent. Throughout the winter a vigorous reassessment of the latters' forces, their equipment, and their thinking had taken place – and in the process several well respected leaders had bowed out – amongst them Guderian and Rundstedt. In the world of the Panzer divisions, technical reassessment had been most necessary whereas tactical doctrine withstood examination since it had prevailed in just about every imaginable circumstance.

Ever since the T-34s and KV 1s had been met, the search for a German tank capable of defeating those two excellent machines had been given urgent priority. At first the German tank soldiers had asked if T-34 could be copied, but this course had to be rejected because German industry did not possess the facilities to reproduce the sort of armour or the light alloy diesel engine that made the T-34 so potent. It will be remembered that as far back as 1937 and 1939, studies had begun on the introduction of radically more powerful medium and heavy tanks, but these had hung fire and by the middle of 1941 had barely reached the prototype stage. However, by then even the prototypes were out of date, since clearly it was no longer a matter of *matching* the T-34; the next German tanks must be a leap ahead of their immediate rival, in order to be at least as good as the next generation of Russian tank likely to be substituted for T-34. So revised designs for a new medium and a heavy tank were pressed ahead in an atmosphere close to panic.

Meanwhile stop-gaps were needed.

**Winter warfare –
Abandoned tanks frozen into the snow**

Fortunately experiments in putting more powerful guns in the existing Mark IIIs and IVs were well ahead, since from the earliest days, both Guderian and Hitler had desired a long 50mm gun on the Mark III. Now their wish had to be granted in haste, while Mark IV was given a long 75mm and both machines fitted with thicker frontal armour. These measures went far to restore the balance of tank power to the German favour. Moreover, assault and tank hunting vehicles mounting the more powerful anti-tank guns in obsolete tank chassis now acquired an increasingly vital importance, for a new gun was often ready for service before a suitable tank could be produced that could carry it in its turret. In any case, assault vehicles were easier and cheaper to produce than tanks, and though the inflexibility of their gun mounting imposed disadvantages in attack, they filled gaps in the infantry's anti-tank defence and thus made that type of formation less liable to cry for help from Panzer

Bale-out from a burning tank

divisions. So, although the assault vehicles were still not issued to the Panzer divisions, they were complementary to them as well as being in competition for the spare parts needed to keep each running.

But the unreliability of German tanks on the Russian front persisted. Decentralised servicing began to make inroads into the backlog of repairs, but the shortage of spares often prevented the Field Workshops from working at full capacity. The overloaded tank industry had never been asked to provide sufficient spares for a long campaign, since this would incur a cut-back in new production. But because constant demands for increased tank production were being made, the provision of spare parts got even worse. Throughout the winter of 1941/42, Hitler, obsessed with quantity rather than quality, urged the formation of more new Panzer divisions in Germany to the detriment of those wasting away in Russia. But the shortages of spares led at last, in May 1942, to a decision to cut back tank production so that more spares could be made available. Either way, units both at the front and in course of formation were starved below full strength, with inevitable tactical consequences, while frequent changes in industrial policy – above all the laying down of new production lines for new models in place of the old ones – caused still further disruption.

Meanwhile, the fitters were driven to extremes of improvisation, the cannibalisation of worn-out equipment in transit from the front for refurbishing in Germany becoming so rampant that quite often only the hull, stripped of all components, reached the base factory. The winter saw the worst of it, but spring came quickly. What might happen then lay in the hands of Hitler, the weather, and incipient Russian recovery, but a certain amount also depended on the demands of other fronts.

The desert
Armour in control

Exposed at the end of the most tenuous Axis supply line of all, Rommel's Afrika Korps had been the first to suffer from the difficulties of maintaining their vehicles in readiness for action. Not until May 1942 were its two Panzer divisions (5th Light had now been rechristened 21st Panzer without receiving a worthwhile increase to its strength) given delivery of their fourth company of tanks in each battalion. It became a matter of concern (but also of internal pride) that from the very beginning, Afrika Korps survived by its own ingenuity – and largely off recovered equipment, friendly and enemy. In this theatre, where reinforcements inevitably lost a sizeable proportion sunk in transit at sea, God helped the Germans who helped themselves, be it from the stocks of British foes or Italian allies.

Foremost in everybody's minds who fought in the desert in 1941 and 1942, was the condition of the fortress of Tobruk. The British wanted to relieve it and, at the same time, destroy Afrika Korps; Rommel wanted to take it as the essential preliminary before finally settling with the British in Egypt. Both Germans and British raced to be the first to put their respective plans into action, and both managed to be ready in the last half of November 1941. It was the British, with their Operation 'Crusader', who got in the first blow, swinging wide round the desert flank and making for Tobruk with three searching, armoured columns. This came as a surprise to Rommel. He had led a rather ponderous raid at the head of 21st Panzer Division towards the British positions in Egypt during September and had failed to detect signs of preparations for an offensive – which was hardly surprising in view of his use of the better part of a Panzer division on a mere reconnaissance. He might have been better advised to try to emulate the proven success of the light scouting parties employed by the British Long Range Desert Group.

When the British struck, Rommel was on the verge of assaulting Tobruk, his two Panzer divisions being concentrated to the east of the port from

The controller – Erwin Rommel

Operation Crusader 1941

- ◄ Attacks by British Eighth Army
- ▨ Positions held by 21st & 15th Panzer Divisions
- ▦ Italian positions
- ➡ Rommel's frontier raid Nov 24/28
- – – – Approximate front lines Nov 18, 1941

where they could intervene should the British try to sally out of Egypt to the aid of the besieged. His deployment was therefore admirably suited to the coming battle, although only the presence of a number of long, field-mounted 50mm anti-tank guns (which could cope with every type of British tank including the Matilda) armed Rommel any better than in June. Thus the Germans took the lead in the gun/armour race in the desert, although in quantity the British were far ahead, fielding 756 tanks (with many more in reserve) against the combined force of 569 German and Italian tanks.

But the British used their armoured brigades dispersed while the Germans fought concentrated, throwing Afrika Korps into action with both Panzer divisions united on more than one crucial occasion. Throughout a week's hard pounding and highly complex manoeuvring to the south of Tobruk in the vicinity of Sidi Rezegh, Afrika Korps succeeded in taking on each British armoured formation in turn and defeating them in detail.

These tank battles were small beer compared with the gigantic encounters in Russia, but because they were localised they served to highlight the tones of tank warfare more subtly than with the bigger displays elsewhere. Consequently they could be analysed more readily and the lessons disseminated in an instant. Fire fights took place at the maximum possible range commensurate with a deceptive visibility. The standard of

shooting by both sides left much to be desired, but superior optics and a technique of firing from stationary positions rather than on the move, as the British often tried to do, gave the German tank gunners an edge. Even so, the number of casualties from battle damage were lower than those incurred by breakdown; the wildly fluctuating tank states of both contenders reflected the efforts of the repair parties as much as the destruction wrought by gunners. Hence, in a battle of constant motion in which the occupation of all but the most commanding or tank-proof ground was a secondary consideration, tank casualties littered the desert. Therefore the occupation of tank graveyards by repair teams could be claimed as a victory: conversely, to foresake an area known to be full of dead enemy tanks without either towing them away or blowing them up was a tactical sin.

Rommel committed a tactical sin as he reached the point of executing a *coup de grace* upon the British. Had he continued to grind down the British at Sidi Rezegh for another 24 hours on 24th November, total victory might have been his. Instead he elected to carry out a grandiose sweep along the Egyptian frontier aimed at the British communications, and, in so doing, left the shaken British to patch up great numbers of their broken tanks lying about the scene of their recent reverse. British prospects were restored by default, for not only did Rommel's frontier raid give the British a chance to recuperate, it also plunged his own forces into a confusion compounded by his personal loss of control of the battle: in the process the Panzer divisions suffered casualties they could not afford. So, although the battle continued for another fortnight in the approaches to Tobruk (and was illuminated by the repeated local successes of the Panzer divisions in collaboration with the Italians), the final outcome was an Axis defeat. Rommel's tank strength was depleted and his supplies exhausted – only by a fighting retreat to El Agheila could he escape total destruction.

Here, as in Russia, the German soldiers fought most valiantly and resourcefully in adversity. The entry of America into the war on the Allied side seemed to introduce no immediate debilitative effect on morale, even though its portent in a war of material can hardly have escaped the notice and fears of those who apprehended the meaning of American industrial potential. Setbacks and disappointments never seemed to disturb the German soldiers' confidence in themselves or their leaders. On the retreat they would turn to snap defiantly at their pursuers, extracting a disproportionate toll from the enemy on each occasion. And once at the furthest limit of their withdrawal, they got busy preparing for a comeback, springing eastward once again in mid-January with an offensive in which tanks and anti-tank guns co-operated in the attack as never before.

The very success of the German counteroffensive sprang from this ability of the Panzer divisions to adapt themselves to new conditions, as opposed to opponents who seemed to spend their time labouring under instruction. There was an evolutionary continuity in German methods that could not be found so strongly amongst the British – a continuity that may have sprung, in part, from the length of time the German commanders, from Rommel downwards, retained their appointments. Very few German leaders were sacked, although a great many were knocked out in action because they habitually moved and worked in the front line.

Rommel's new offensive prospered. By the end of January the British had been ejected from Benghazi, their forces in the forward zone largely destroyed by the Germans without Italian assistance. In consternation the British main body retired, this time to an artificial defensive position at Gazala, screening the approaches to the forward base at Tobruk.

As viewed by Rommel, the desert war could not continue much longer as it had been doing. Each local success enjoyed by Afrika Korps seemed only to defer British recovery; Rommel knew about the vast supplies of material pouring into Africa from America and the United Kingdom, and that, unless he won a complete victory in the near future, Afrika

Korps must inevitably be overwhelmed. For he also guessed that a time must come when the British evolved a tactical technique that matched his own. Up to mid-1942 each Axis battle in Africa had been of a defensive or spoiling nature – the counter to Operation 'Crusader' a splendid example of the former, the riposte to Gazala a calculated instance of the latter. Now Rommel planned to rid the North African shores of British influence for ever by defeating the British at Gazala, capturing Tobruk and then driving east to seize the Suez Canal Base deep in Egypt – despite Hitler's instructions that, after Tobruk had fallen, the offensive was to be stopped in favour of an invasion of Malta to prevent it dominating Rommel's seaward lines of communication.

Rommel launched his attack on 26th May, 1942, depending, as usual, upon his Panzer divisions stealing a gambler's victory on the assumption that the British armour would be no more powerful and no better handled than on any previous occasion. Realising that the British had constructed a necklace of defended infantry localities strung together amongst minefields from the coast to Bir Hakeim, Rommel sought to outflank the entire position by swinging his armour round its southern extremity prior to rushing the British armour base installations grouped in rear. Rommel's forecast of his opponents' reactions was wholly perspicacious for the British committed their armour piecemeal in the same old way. But with regard to comparative technical quality his forecasts were exploded, when, almost at once, his tanks ran into the better armed and armoured American Grant tank (then in service with the British Army for the first time) and then against the first of the British 6-pounder guns guns (equivalent of his own 50mm anti-tank guns). Then on top of that there occurred an awful muddle amongst minefields of appalling density.

Because the leading German troops had the worst of a fight with the Grants and because insufficient enemy supplies were captured, protracted operations could no longer be guaranteed since execution of the original plan depended on captures of that kind. On 30th May, it was clear that Rommel had failed to defeat the British armour, had run short of supplies, and could only live hand-to-mouth on the enemy side of a defended minefield where he survived in the hope that a lane might be cleared for his supply columns in the nick of time. In the meantime the surprise discovery of a British infantry 'box' blocking the course of the projected lane through the minefield lowered Afrika Korps' chances to a precarious level.

The operations that followed represent an essential stage in the development of armoured technique. Rommel assumed that the British would waste no time in throwing everything they possessed against his tight defensive position – called the 'Cauldron' – where it faced north, east, and south on the British side of the minefields. Without any alternative (since he had insufficient petrol to take him south round Bir Hakeim to safety) Rommel stood on the defensive in the forlorn hope that the British might destroy themselves in vain attacks against his anti-tank guns. He was not to visualise that a slow and diffuse British reaction would fail to co-ordinate a full-blown counterattack, or that he would be given time to cut through the minefield without hindrance. In fact, those British attacks which did reach into the Cauldron left the Panzer divisions unshaken at further cost to the British tank force. At one moment Rommel had seriously considered the prospect of abject surrender due to shortage of drinking water. But a few days later he was strong enough to break out from the Cauldron to threaten the British army to the west of Tobruk and then Tobruk itself, impelling the British to launch improvised attacks against the Panzer divisions where the Germans fought on ground of their own choosing. In essence, the tactics practised by Rommel's Panzer divisions were strictly of an offensive defensive character. Armour and anti-tank guns would be pushed through to

Air co-operation. A Stuka is given its target

occupy ground that was vital to the enemy: against that ground the enemy would be lured to destruction upon screens of guns backed up by the mobile body of tanks.

In this way the British armour was persuaded to destroy itself at Gazala, and the British tank force (which had started the battle with a considerable superiority in numbers) written down to such an extent that it could neither protect the infantry in Tobruk nor mount a credible mobile defence of the Egyptian frontier. Without armour in a desert campaign there is no salvation. Tobruk fell to Afrika Korps on 21st June, an event celebrated by Rommel with a request to Hitler that the Malta plan should be dropped in favour of a headlong pursuit of the broken British into Egypt – the sort of temptation that the opportunism of Hitler and Mussolini could not resist. On 30th June the Panzer divisions had thrown the British out of their long prepared defences at Mersa Matruh with hardly a struggle (largely because of a mis-understanding amongst the British leaders who withdrew prematurely just when the Germans had reached the point of exhaustion). Next stop was the British defensive system at El Alamein.

British and Germans from Matruh arrived at El Alamein in close asso-ciation, the British in a muddle, the Germans mixed up with some of the retreating British – all concerned living close to the point of physical collapse. German tank strengths were not more than 50, their supplies and lorries, along with a proportion of the artillery, were British. In fact, the tired Panzer divisions of Afrika Korps had achieved remarkable efficiency in improvisation and diversification, but, unfortunately for them, they had soon to contend with fresh, properly equipped British forces in addition to those that wended their way back to Egypt in company with Afrika Korps. And so the battle reached stalemate in the 40 mile gap that lay between the Mediterranean Sea and the salt marsh of Qattara.

Few German tanks in Africa had not undergone some sort of major

Pz Kw IV F2
In a whole variety of marks, Pz Kw IV remained in service with Panzer Divisions
throughout the war, up-gunned and up-armoured by stages in order to compete
with each enemy technical advance. This version has the L/48 75mm gun that
made it a match for the Russian T34/76 and the American Sherman. Weight 23 tons.
Speed: 25 mph. Crew: five. 1 x 75mm gun, 2 x 7.9 mm mg.

battlefield repair at some time in their career – and many were veterans of frequent workshop visits. Their crews too were at the end of their tether, so the attritional battles that gusted to and fro in the Alamein position from July until November were a technician and tactician's nightmare. The subsequent July battles sprang from British efforts to destroy Afrika Korps while it hung on at the extremities of over-long communications before it could recover its wind after the pursuit. But whereas previous British offensives had tended to aim direct blows at the Panzer divisions, they now went out of the way to attack anything rather than the German armour, concentrating instead on the 'soft' Italian infantry formations in the hope that the Germans would break their tanks in abortive counterattacks aimed at restoring Italian fortunes. Quite often this came about in a battle that struggled at a reduced tempo. Not only were both sides extremely tired, they also found that the minefields, being in crazy and multiplying confusion all over the battlefield, con-

gealed movement almost as effectively as the mud of the Russian steppe. At first, desert minefields were looked on as a local phenomenon, but gradually they became a fundamental tactical feature that put a new complexion on armoured warfare as the Germans turned more to defence.

The battle dwindled to a skirmish until the end of August. Both sides built up their strength – what little reinforcement the Germans received being in the shape of a few of the up-gunned, up-armoured Mark IV tanks that had originally been designed as a counter to the Russian T-34. On 30th August, Rommel tried once again to dislodge the British from El Alamein, aiming a stroke at the British rear where it held the ridge at Alam Halfa. He failed, not only because the British dug in too strongly in a vital position that their new commander, General Montgomery, knew must be attacked, but because there were no Axis reserves of petrol sufficient to sustain prolonged operations. Concealed British tanks and anti-tank guns expelled each attack – not least because their direction was

A newcomer to the gun armour race – the Grant tank

circumscribed and channelled into predictable lines. From overhead, the British Air Force soaked the German supply lines in high explosive. Within less than a week the German offensive had fallen back, more or less, whence it had come.

The effects of this reverse on German fortunes in North Africa, considered in conjunction with what was going on in Russia (of which more later), were incalculable. Rommel had been defeated for the first time and in quick time. Deprived of adequate support at the end of an overextended supply line, he appreciated that, not only had he met an enemy in possession of superior material, but, with great reluctance, one whose tactics blunted his own. For three years Panzer divisions, because they practised unique methods that were technically and psychologically superior to those of any other army, had run rings round every foe. Throughout that victorious era the Luftwaffe had provided complementary support essential for softening the strongest enemy resistance, for preventing enemy aircraft from dis-rupting or even overseeing German movements and, on occasion, for supplying forward troops with materials in short supply. Against the British and the Americans, those days were over and Rommel, who seemed to be in the habit of sampling the first taste of each new hostile development, was the first to suggest that the sort of defence crippling him in the desert, might soon cripple Panzer divisions on every other front.

It is hardly surprising that the German High Command (at that moment immersed in an huge offensive deep in the Caucasus and, so it seemed, on the verge of annihilating the Russians) paid not the slightest attention. They continued to view the Western Desert as a special case where the lessons had no universal application. At this time the Germans were so uplifted by success as the supreme, world military power, that criticism from anybody (let alone an upstart from their own side), came discordantly amiss. The very success of the Panzer divisions had inculcated an overwhelming and dangerous conceit amongst the German hierarchy.

El Agheila to El Alamein 1942

Rommel returned home in September a sick man in need of convalescence, leaving behind a defensive framework accepted by his successor as the only logical method of waging a battle within strictly economical lines. The Axis front was held by infantry amongst deep minefields with the Panzer divisions kept in rear, amalgamated with Italian armoured divisions, as an insurance against the instability of the latter. However, in order to counter enemy penetrations in the least possible time before they could be exploited, the Axis armour was kept much closer to the front than normal and, of greater significance, told to fight only on the ground within their immediate boundaries. This curtailment came about quite simply in order to conserve petrol: movement had to be forbidden in all but the most urgent cases.

Tactics such as these were obviously foreign to the optimum use of Panzer divisions, as was discovered when the battle blossomed out on 23rd October and it was found that the infantry-biased attritional warfare practised by Montgomery, in which armour played only a subsidiary role behind rolling artillery and aerial bombardments, wore away the Panzer divisions without commensurate returns. In addition, the advent of the new American built Sherman tank, with its 75mm gun capable of firing high-explosive (as well as armour piercing) shells, made it possible for the British tank crews to engage exposed 88mm guns on something like equal terms for the first time. Remorselessly the Axis infantry positions were torn to bits, compelling the Panzer divisions to fill the vacuum thus created. So, though the Panzer divisions had to move but a short distance, inevitable destruction rewarded their attempts to fight within constricted limits without the option of free manoeuvre.

Rommel returned to Africa to pilot his men through their most testing time; simultaneously one of the original German tank pioneers – General von Thoma – commanded Afrika Korps at the front. But at last not even Rommel could stem the British pressure, so, as the front began to disintegrate, he sent both Panzer divisions (with all 50 tanks) mobile into the desert as a last resort, draining away the last petrol as they went. And in due course not even the Hitler 'no retreat' formula could save them (in fact it put Afrika Korps in even greater jeopardy): a fighting withdrawal nearly became a rout as the remnants of the Axis forces decanted into the open desert protected from pursuit by only a thin screen of armour under Thoma. But once Thoma had fallen captive, Rommel could only just keep ahead of a hot pursuit, repeatedly in danger of being overrun – usually when petrol supplies failed – but never completely out of control.

It was mid-November when the Panzer divisions quitted Egypt for the last time, their retreat the most precipitate of any German withdrawal up to then. But soon they were seen to be merely setting the tone. German fortunes had turned irrevocably into decline.

A Pz Kw III and its target

ursuit to Alamein

Stalingrad
Death of an elite

Counter-attack in the snow

Writing after the war, Mellenthin, a highly qualified Panzer staff officer with experience in the French, African and Russian theatres of war, gave it as his considered opinion that, whereas air power had played an influential part in the Western theatre of war, the enormous fronts and the relatively small scale of the air effort, limited the effects of air power on the Russian Front. 'There', wrote Mellenthin, 'tank armies were the main instrument of victory'.

Knowing this too, the Russians grouped their armour and best troops to guard against yet another attempt by the Germans to take Moscow in the summer of 1942, and flung many to destruction in an abortive offensive against Kharkov in May. Then, while Rommel chased the British back into Egypt, the exhausted Russians detected a large build-up of German armour south of Bryansk – and assumed that this must be part of a force destined to strike northwards for their capital. They were utterly mistaken, for this concentration was none other than General Hoth's

Fourth Panzer Army, the northern flank of Army Group South's supreme effort – and, indeed, the main effort of the entire Wehrmacht –aimed at breaking through west of the River Don as a prelude to debouching into the Caucasus in a feverish rush for oil. Once again Hitler's objectives were political and economic, for some said later that the very name of the city of Stalingrad on the River Volga attracted the German dictator's ambitions, while Hitler himself left nobody in doubt that, if the Panzer armies failed to seize the oilfields near Maikop, the tanks in which they drove would soon no longer have fuel on which to run.

So, after the usual winter contretemps over future plans, Army Group South set off into the Caucasian foothills, its Army Group A told to make for Rostov and then to cross the Don on the way to Maikop (with Kleist's First Panzer Army in the lead), while Army Group B, comprising Hoth's Fourth Panzer Army and Paulus's Sixth Army (including a Panzer corps) strove to charge down the right bank

The victor of Kharkov –
General von Manstein

General Hoth

of the Don, past Voronezh, towards Stalingrad. Thus Army Group B had, as its first priority, the defeat of the Russian forces guarding the Voronezh Front and thereafter a task as flank guard to Army Group A's southward plunge. This they could accomplish by extending along the Don – as far as Stalingrad if necessary – but without making Stalingrad their principal objective. In Army Group B, Fourth Panzer Army took the lead. It will be noticed that the amorphous term Panzer 'group' had been dropped, an indication that the Panzers were no longer subservient to 'Army'. Indeed, Sixth Army was scheduled to play second fiddle to Fourth Panzer Army, merely taking over ground after the latter had driven ahead. Furthermore, once Fourth Panzer Army's divisions had reached all their objectives, it was to revert into reserve, ready to cope with the Russian counter thrusts which all knew must eventually be directed southward across the Don as the best way to take the Germans' Caucasian venture in rear.

Abortive Russian attacks on the Kharkov front in May had already seriously weakened their offensive capability with the result that they could neither hold nor strike back at Fourth Panzer Army when it erupted towards Voronezh on 28th June. The ensuing battles were not even reminiscent of those in 1941; veterans in the Panzer army actually compared them with those of 1939 in Poland, so complete was the Russian collapse and the German mastery. With the bit between their teeth Hoth's tankmen (many of whom had been cavalrymen before the war) raced flat out for Voronezh. Thereupon they were meant to turn south-east down the Don without bothering to cross the river. But finding a bridge over the river unblown, one tank company leader, strongly imbued with the cavalry spirit, dashed across, followed in quick time by the rest of the tank battalion and then a whole Panzer division.

So fast raced the tanks that neither Russians nor Germans could keep track of them, so while the Russians suffered annihilation in many areas, in others, notably within the bends of the river, pockets or bridgeheads were bypassed and then overlooked by Sixth Army bringing up the German rear. General Paulus's Sixth Army travelled mainly on horse and foot and could not hope to keep up with Hoth's Panzers. Hoth claimed that had he been given a free rein he could have taken Stalingrad on the run by the end of July. So while the Panzers stretched ahead of the infantry, the infantry expended their strength in eliminating some of the enemy Don pockets which had been bypassed by the Panzers, but left others to simmer.

In the meantime Army Group A had failed to do quite as well as its left-hand neighbour, principally because more opposition than expected came from amongst the coal-mines and slagheaps scarring the countryside between Rostov and the River Donets. Unhappily this prompted Hitler to alter his original directive in order to deflect Fourth Panzer Army to assist Kleist's First Panzer Army across the Don, leaving Sixth Army to take over where Fourth Panzer Army left off in its advance to Stalingrad. Numerous side issues developed. Kleist not only crossed the Don without assistance, but had reason to complain that the arrival of Fourth Panzer Army in his immediate vicinity badly clogged the already overloaded supply routes. Sixth Army, set a task beyond its means, could not move with the same freedom as the Panzers and thus gave the Russians more time to fill the yawning gap that, for a while, spread tantalisingly open to the west of Stalingrad. From then on, resistance to Sixth Army hardened and had reached formidable proportions even before the Volga city had come into view on 20th August. The entire situation had been altered.

Sending Fourth Panzer Army on a wild-goose-chase not only thwarted the drive to Stalingrad and got in Kleist's way, it also dissipated Army Group B's mobile reserve: moreover, its arrival on the lower Don compressed 75% of the entire German tank strength in Russia into one small arena, causing the servicing organisation to break down once more because spare parts could not be ferried down the choked roads. As the countryside became littered with immobilised machines, fighting strengths wilted just when they were most needed at full strength. And as Kleist thrust almost unopposed towards Stavroprol and Maikop, Hitler's ego re-awoke to demand that Stalingrad must be overcome at a faster rate than Sixth Army seemed capable of doing. So thence the willing Fourth Panzer Army had to return.

The stage was now set for the twin battles of the Caucasus and Stalingrad. Kleist's First Panzer Army continued to make staggeringly good progress in its quest for oil, even though the Russians set fire to the Maikop oilfields long before his arrival. The Russians on this front had collapsed, reducing their resistance to that of local skirmishes by desperate men who were literally defending their own homes. Hitler told Kleist to make for Baku when to the Panzer soldiers the grand finale looked almost in sight, causing a wave of optimism to sweep their ranks as they roared forward almost unimpeded mile after mile.

But in the approaches to Stalingrad, where the same peace-happy atmosphere at first pervaded, signs of a psychological malaise that matched the failing mechanical health of the tanks became apparent. It was noticed that 'The German tanks did not go into action without infantry and air support. On the battlefield there was no evidence of the 'prowess' of German tank crews ... they operated sluggishly, extremely cautiously and indecisively.' In other words, with victory round the corner, a natural inclination to stay alive in order to enjoy the promised peace came to the surface – the opposite of the spirit that had motivated the Germans in Poland.

On 22nd August, XIV Panzer Corps forced its way into the northern outskirts of Stalingrad, expecting, perhaps, that the entire river bank might be cleared as a formality – the more so since military logic would denounce the Russians for fighting with their backs to a wide river. The Sixth Army closed up to the city from the east while Fourth Panzer Army drove the Russians away from its southern environs. The First Panzer Army continued to roam the Caucasus. Everywhere, except close to the Panzer spearhead tips, in the suburbs and along the supply routes to Stalingrad, the Germans and their Rumanian, Hungarian, and Italian allies were perilously thin on the ground. Infantry divisions screening the flanks of the wide corridor leading to the panzer front sometimes watched territory that stretched over 40 miles, a condition that might have been more acceptable had there been a mobile tank reserve on reasonably quick call. But the Panzer divisions were all in the line, the most unfortunate and misemployed among them in the process of being sucked into the torn streets of Stalingrad.

On the banks of the Volga the Russians fought to the death and, as is celebrated, never relaxed their hold on its eastern sector. Thence Stalin and Hitler fed thousands of men and mountains of munitions, grinding each other's soldiers into pulp in a head-on clash such as the Germans, at any rate, had carefully avoided up to then. Bit by bit, and day by day, Hitler converted Stalingrad into a personal test of strength between Stalin and himself – and in so doing reversed his strategic aims, since this attack could only be sustained by extracting vital elements from Army Group A in the Caucasus. Soon Kleist was complaining that every scrap of Luftwaffe support except for reconnaissance aircraft had been withdrawn from him. At the end of lengthening lines of communication he lacked bombers (the Panzers' heavy artillery) and airborne logistic transports. All had gone to pound Stalingrad. He had wielded his Panzers with consummate ease in the classic manner, switching their efforts from one line of advance to another in a scintillating criss-cross of manoeuvres designed to delude, surprise, and evade the Russian defenders. Now the vast scale of his movements at the extremities of over-extended supply lines brought him to a halt from lack of support and from petrol shortage on ground where untapped oil might be found in tons beneath his feet.

Diametrically opposed to Kleist's employment of Panzer divisions was their use by Paulus at Stalingrad. Caught in the vice of Hitler's egoism,

he had no alternative, short of resignation (and Paulus was not the resigning sort), other than to break all the canons of Panzer law, and throw the tanks and armoured personnel-carriers into the whirl of street combat. But if Paulus did not mind losing so many irreplaceable armoured soldiers on wasteful tasks to which they were totally unsuited, the generals commanding XV and IV Panzer Corps did. Both Wittersheim and Schwedler protested volubly – both were sacked. And still the slaughter of tanks went on in the

Panzer Grenadiers stand-by to help the ta

midst of a battle which, first, had no place in German strategy and, second, belonged to the realms of infantry – and also fantasy. Then looming over them all, appeared a growing Russian threat from the unprotected flanks against the exposed rear of Sixth Army and Fourth Panzer Army at Stalingrad as, for the first time, the Russians beheld their enemy fixed in a position that invited the sort of mobile counterstroke at which the Germans themselves excelled. Then the autumn mud came to hamper movement, and later froze to give new life to mobility.

From out of the Don bridgeheads that had remained in Russian hands after the German advance to Stalingrad, and from the steppe to the south of the city itself, four Russian Tank corps debouched on 19th November. Each blow fell on sub-standard Rumanian divisions whose fronts were held lighter than prudence allowed. Penetrations were made at once with a momentum of Germanic velocity, building up as the Russians exploited their advantage deep into German-held territory with a verve and

thoroughness that epitomised the method which they copied from the German Panzer divisions. Now that the tactics were being put to use against their originators with such effect, even the best armour in the Wehrmacht could not prevail. The depleted Panzer divisions in Fourth Panzer Army failed to counter the double envelopment of Stalingrad, when those to the south of the city were destroyed or brushed aside and those closer to its limits driven pell-mell inside the perimeter enclosing Sixth Army amongst the ruins created

by three months' fighting. The Sixth Army, with part of Fourth Panzer Army, entered a state of siege on 23rd November – some 200,000 men, with battered equipment and desperately sparse supplies, cut off from the rest of Army Group South by Russian lines of circumvallation that reached a depth of some 40 miles.

Outside the pocket, General Hoth strove to reconstitute Fourth Panzer Army from survivors, the crews of broken-down tanks and men returning from leave. The overall command of relief operations was entrusted to Field-Marshal von Manstein as Commander, Army Group Don. With Sixth Army, Fourth Panzer Army, Rumanian Third Army, plus an organisation called Group Hollidt, Manstein had somehow to extract Sixth Army and co-ordinate the operation with those of Army Groups A and B on his left and right hands. But the key to any hope of success that might be achieved continued to be, as ever, the combat value of the Panzer divisions. They alone of German formations had a passing chance of cutting a way through the Russian cordon: but they were now weaker than at any time in their existence and the Russians seemed to have learnt how to defeat them at last.

Down in the Caucasus First Panzer Army waited on events, having sent LVII Panzer Corps to help form Manstein's relief force. The Russian incursion at Stalingrad did not yet threaten the retreat of Kleist's men, but would do so if pushed further south-west: meanwhile Hitler forbade him to retreat from the furthest extremity of his holdings close to Mozdok.

As flank guard to First Panzer Army 3rd Panzer Division became aware, on December 5th, of a steady build-up by Russian forces to the east. Upon receiving orders to attack, a battle-group consisting of two tank companies, an infantry company mounted in armoured carriers, and two reconnaissance platoons supported by a battery of self-propelled 105mm howitzers, advanced 7 miles, unopposed, over wide open steppe in search of the enemy. It discovered some Russian infantry just before nightfall and overcame them, but later still more Russians were reported further east.

Self-Propelled Field Howitzer – 'Wasp'
The most common SP artillery in use with Panzer Divisions in the latter part of the war, it replaced the earlier towed, unarmoured pieces that had found difficulty surviving the heat of a mobile armoured battle. The chassis is that of Pz Kw II. Weight: 12 tons. Speed: 25 mph. Crew: five. 1 x 105mm Field Howitzer with a 10° traverse each way

Next morning the Germans advanced again with their tank companies on the right and their infantry on the left. Almost immediately, the enemy engaged them from the front attracting the attention of every tank commander in that direction, so that the sudden appearance of 15 Russian tanks unexpectedly from dead ground to play heavy fire upon the flank of the German group went unnoticed – and cost the Germans several casualties. But having achieved a brilliant initial advantage, the Russians then threw it away by declining to follow up. Thus they demonstrated, in miniature, a partial comprehension of German method that stopped short of actual implementation at the lowest levels. On a far larger scale, as the Russians collected ever bigger armies and directed them to the main arena, the surprise experiences of 3rd Panzer Division were felt by the whole of Army Group Don.

By 12th December a relief force of three Panzer divisions along with units of the Rumanian Fourth Army had been assembled near Kotelnikovo, some 80 miles from the nearest point on Sixth Army's perimeter. It had been hoped to do so a week previously, but LVII Panzer Corps had taken that much longer to move up from the Caucasus. Meanwhile, on both flanks of the relief force, the Russians endeavoured to extend the depth of their south-westerly penetration in order to pinch out the relieving force even before it started on its obvious predestined way. Complex tank battles raged behind the River Chir where German infantry held the river line, after Russian tanks had broken through, leaving the penetrations to be countered in depth by 11th Panzer Division operating *behind* their own infantry's front. In these tense situations the best infantry formations could do was maintain their existing positions, seal the gaps through which the Russians had driven, and hope that the Panzer divisions would destroy the Russian incursion. This time, on the Chir, 11th Panzer, by superior tactics, worked the miracle.

Near Kotelnikovo Manstein's relief attempt overran Russian forces that were themselves outstretched, and for nearly a week pressed back the enemy

The advance to the Caucasus and Stalingrad 1942

Map legend:
- ► Panzer Armies
- ▻ Infantry Armies
- --- Front line Nov 18, 1942
- — Front line June 28

until the gap separating the Panzer divisions from Stalingrad measured only 23 miles. And then, in the face of further massive Russian reinforcements which could not be budged, the Germans stopped, exhausted, sealing the fate of Stalingrad and with it the sterling elements of three Panzer divisions which could never be replaced. Soon the gap separating the besieged from the relief had been widened to hopeless dimensions, for on 24th December, the Russians renewed violent and well directed armoured attacks that not only eliminated Manstein's hard won gains, but expanded the frontage of the original assault wide to its flanks. This Russian offensive aimed at nothing less than the total isolation of every German formation east of the Don – in other words, the best part of the waning Panzer force.

The struggle between German and Russian armoured formations grew daily more violent and on a scale greater than ever before. Hordes of Russian tanks, well directed from the top but poorly guided at the lower levels, raced, regardless of losses, to close the corridor held open by Manstein to the east of Rostov through which First Panzer Army ran to escape

from the Caucasus. One vast strategic collision overscored a thousand desperate tactical conflicts from Army Group to section level, spreading from one end of the front to the other. Since both sides now employed almost identical tactics (even though the Russians used far greater numbers) the game of thrust and counter-thrust assumed an almost stereotyped outline, thrown into relief at those points where German companies and crews with superior training enjoyed the best of an encounter. A torrent of Russian tanks would usually pour across the rolling steppe, its entrance heralded by heavy artillery and aerial bombardment. In its path the tightly stretched German infantry, bolstered by assault-guns, would perform mainly as an early warning system that was barely capable of absorbing the first enemy onrush amongst a network of 'hedgehogs' set in scattered villages and woods. Pockets of resistance, the size of armies down to isolated companies, would collect and resist, while the faithful Panzer divisions wove their patterns in efforts to wear down the roving Russian tank hordes, decimate their infantry, intercept supplies (even though it was difficult to be sure whether these self-sufficient attackers bothered to carry any with them), and rescue those units that could no longer hold out behind the enemy lines. To soldiers who later fought in the closer confines of Europe, the scope for manoeuvre on the Russian steppe was inconceivable. Only big minds that thought at speed with acute perception and clinical accuracy could master the detail and cool boldness required. For a long time a solid bank of experience saved the Germans since they could outthink all but the top Russian commanders of the stamp of Marshal Zhukov, and sense the exact moment when, having run out of steam, the Russians lay vulnerable to a counterblow.

In February 1943, after the Russian Sixth Army had pressed open a wide bulge south of Kharkov towards the River Dniepr at Dnepropetrovsk, it looked as if their hurrying spearheads were in difficulty. Kursk had fallen, as had Kharkov – both of them important route centres – and Hitler had

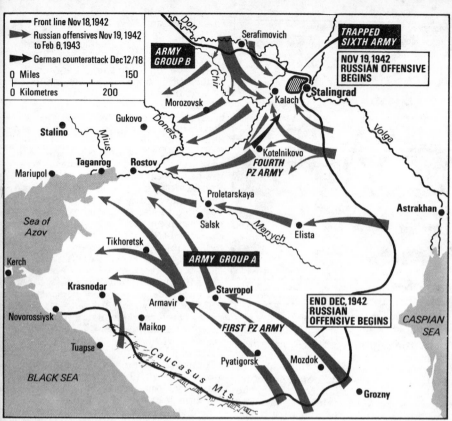

The Russian counter- attack at Stalingrad 1942–1943

Russian T34 in Stalingrad

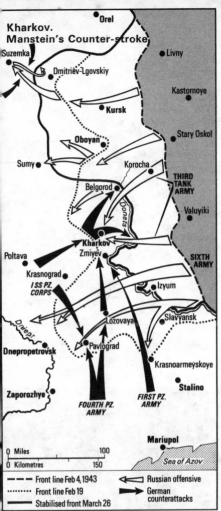

Kharkov.
Manstein's Counter-stroke

Orel	
Livny	
Suzemka	
Dmitriev-Lgovskiy	
Kastornoye	
Kursk	
Oboyan	
Stary Oskol	
Sumy	
Korocha	
Belgorod	THIRD TANK ARMY
Valuyiki	
Kharkov	
Zmiyёv	SIXTH ARMY
Poltava	
Krasnograd	
I SS PZ. CORPS	Izyum
Slavyansk	
Lozovaya	
Dnepr	
Pavlograd	
Dnepropetrovsk	Krasnoarmeyskoye
Zaporozhye	Stalino
FOURTH PZ. ARMY	FIRST PZ. ARMY
Mariupol	
Sea of Azov	

0 Miles   100
0 Kilometres   150

- - - Front line Feb 4, 1943
········ Front line Feb 19
⎯⎯⎯ Stabilised front March 26

⬅ Russian offensive
➡ German counterattacks

come in person to Manstein's headquarters to urge him to retake Kharkov at once. Manstein had replied that he preferred to let the Russians drop deeper into the trap he was preparing – at one time he actually had Russian tanks in sight of his own headquarters. Coolly throughout February, he wore down the Russian hordes, regrouping his own mobile troops, meanwhile, on the wings of the enemy penetrations. To the north of the Russian drive, I SS Panzer Corps assembled near Krasnograd with orders to thrust south-east through the enemy mass in the direction of Pavlograd, and create the anvil against which five Panzer divisions of

the three Panzer corps of Fourth and First Panzer Armies, were to hammer the counterblow from west of Krasnoarmeyskoye past Lozovaya in the direction of Kharkov.

These concentric blows hit the Russians on 20th February just as they themselves were indulging in a renewed attempt to reach the Dniepr. Moreover, Manstein's gathering of forces had been so skilful that the Russians were fooled into believing that nothing more than a German fighting withdrawal was in progress: it is to the enhancement of well-conducted Panzer operations that a commander's intentions can be disguised by virtue of the fact that the main force need not be taken close to the front until a moment before impact. With impeccable deception and timing, Manstein caught the Russians off balance, short of fuel, and enjoying a false state of security. The tables were completely turned by Panzer divisions which had known no rest or retraining for months on end, and whose tank strength was far below its proper level. The Russians recoiled with the Germans in feverish pursuit, for at any time the spring thaw might well call back the mud and bring all further operations to an end – this was yet another race against time to snatch every possible prize.

In fact the thaw came early that spring, but not before the Germans had cut the Russian Sixth Army and their Third Tank Army to pieces, cleaned up the salient jutting out towards the Dnieper, re-assembled no less than 12 triumphant Panzer divisions to the west of Izyum, and then crashed through to Kharkov and, ultimately, Belgorod. Indeed, but for the thaw and the mud, a third phase planned by Manstein could hardly have failed to cut off the bulge that now jutted on either side of Kursk. But that operation had to wait for a later more propitious occasion. Meanwhile hundreds of Russian tanks and guns lay stranded, many out of fuel, where their crews had abandoned them – though many crewmen escaped across the uninviting steppe to fight another day.

The ice-blasted Steppe

Overload on the repair shops

Infantry amongst the ruins

A rubber-sprung bed

Defeat in Stalingrad

Panzer Division in full flood

The new elite

large and valuable part of the panzer force had been lost at Stalingrad and in the subsequent battles during the winter of 1942-43. Meanwhile, in North Africa, battles with smaller forces engaged, but of no less intensity, had been fought. For even as Rommel withdrew the emaciated remnants of Afrika Korps from El Alamein, a great Anglo-American armada began to land fresh armies in Morocco and Algeria and in quick time these began to move westwards towards their objectives – Tunis and Bizerta. Thus Afrika Korps stood to be caught in a vice between the British advancing from Egypt and the Anglo-American spearheads approaching from Algiers. With troops rushed over from Italy the Axis leaders sought only to hold open a temporary bridgehead around Tunis and Bizerta in which Rommel's army could find sanctuary before being evacuated to Europe. However, such now was Hitler's mania for holding on to every scrap of territory, in next to no time he was exhorting unyielding defence not only in Tunisia and in

Tripolitania, but in almost every wadi as well – a complete negation of copybook armoured tactics. Repeatedly Hitler kept demanding 'no withdrawal' and intervening at the lowest possible levels of command, obliterating the fundamental freedom and flexibility of action drawn from command at the Panzer tip, that lay at the root of the Panzer divisions' triumph. Therefore the German military leaders fought with their eyes on the enemy and their ears and senses tuned to Hitler who injected a distraction such as might cause the enemy to rejoice.

By a process of escalation more and more Axis men and material poured into northern Tunisia, (thus forming Fifth Panzer Army) so that by the end of January, when Afrika Korps reached safety in the southern part of the country behind the defensive position at Mareth, sufficient armour had been accumulated to raise their two Panzer divisions closer to full strength than for months. Added to this, the presence of the strong 10th Panzer Division backed up by one of

The mountains of Tunisia. The leading tank in the foreground is one of the first Tigers in action.

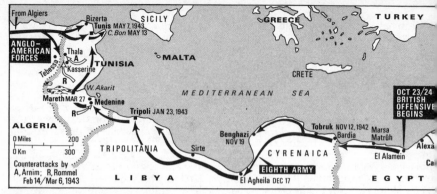

El Alamein to Tunis 1942–1943

the formidable Tiger battalions, made major offensive operations possible instead of minor counterattacks, though it was pretty galling for Rommel's soldiers to witness this parade of strength one half of which a few months back might have carried them to Cairo. Nevertheless they could now join with the fresh tide and pound a new enemy – and one who looked somewhat 'green'.

The Americans held the line to the east of Kasserine Pass with their 1st Armoured Division. North and west of that key bottleneck lay the way to the rear of the Allied armies, then in the process of building up their strength for a final assault against Tunis. For the moment Montgomery's pursuit, short of supplies, had stalled before Mareth. Seizing this opportunity to employ armoured troops as they were meant to be used, General von Arnim, commanding Fifth Panzer Army, threw a sharp local offensive against the American armoured division on 13th February, 1943, and managed to repeat with all three Panzer divisions in North Africa what concentrated Panzer divisions had always achieved against 'green' armies – a total engulfment. Yet, in fact, Arnim's intentions were strictly of a defensive nature – he was not the 'exploiting' kind, whereas Rommel, following up hard with scratch forces to the south of Arnim's victory, visualised the widespread results that might be won by pursuing hard to the north in the grand manner down the line of least expectation towards Tebèssa. But although his desire to exploit was granted, its direction was

veered towards Thala – just where t[...] Allies expected him and had ma[...] ready to receive him. So, within a f[...] days, the offensive died away a[...] Rommel (now placed in command all Axis forces in North Afric[...] reversed course to dart back to Mare[...] and fling all three Panzer divisio[...] against Montgomery's Eighth Arm[...] where it defended Medenine. But, [...] at Alam Halfa, Rommel executed [...] direct predictable attack and w[...] roughly repulsed. And at that he le[...] Africa for good, leaving overall com[...] mand in Arnim's hands.

The rest of the Africa story is brie[...] told from the Panzer divisions' poi[...] of view. With reinforcements stra[...] gled by the blockade sealing th[...] seaway to Sicily, and faced by moun[...] ing attacks from Anglo-American a[...] French forces along the length of a[...] indefensible front, the Germa[...] Italian Armies could delay on[...] tenuously, simply butting their hea[...] against each recurring breakthrou[...] prior to withdrawal to the next line[...] resistance. As usual the Panzer div[...] sions occupied central hides or di[...] persed themselves strategically b[...] hind each threatened front; and [...] usual the Allied commanders trimme[...] their plans to take full account [...] what the Panzer divisions might d[...] both British and Americans fr[...] quently performing far more ca[...] tiously than necessary under t[...] misconception that the Panzer div[...] sions were stronger than they act[...] ally were or were about to comm[...] some act that exceeded the bounds [...] possibility.

From Mareth to Wadi Akarit, a[...]

finally into the mountain ring that guarded the Axis held ports of Tunis and Bizerta, the Panzer divisions shielded the retreating Army until, with their strength at little more than a battlegroup and without sufficient fuel for more than a couple of days, they grouped together and flung one last Wagnerian charge at Djebel Bou Aoukaz just before the last Allied offensive extinguished all Axis military activity in North Africa.

Not unnaturally, the development of Panzer forces ran parallel to the progress of the political organisation that had given them life. The Panzer force, emerging subversively like the Nazi Party, in a series of opportunist convulsions, found its evolution reflecting the fragmentation that epitomised the German nation's organisation and economy. Hitler's preference for his immediate Nazi Party entourage did more than place influence in the hands of unscrupulous men: it led to the birth of private armies, gradually allowing the Military Branch of the SS, the Waffen-SS, to acquire far greater resources than the Wehrmacht, a process copied by Göring with his Luftwaffe divisions.

The Panzer divisions felt this diversification most of all. At first the Waffen-SS had formed only Motorised Infantry Divisions and a single tank regiment, but early in 1943 they began to build their own Panzer divisions (converting the first three from the original SS Motorised or Panzer Grenadier divisions). This formation, as we have seen, took a leading part in Manstein's Kharkov triumph. The SS were, of course, the élite of an élite – the pick of Germany's youth, drafted into prime formations with establishments that were not only larger than those of the conventional Wehrmacht Panzer division (each SS tank battalion had 59 tanks compared to 48 in a Wehrmacht battalion) but maintained closer to full strength with the latest equipment. Moreover, SS commanders stood a better chance of keeping their jobs and their heads than an ordinary army officer when they acted in defiance of Hitler's more outrageous orders. These trends reflected Hitler's long term intention of replacing the military hierarchy with a para-military élite imbued with political loyalty – and what more appropriate place to expand than at the core of the field army.

Amongst Hitler's favourites congregated designers and engineers whose more outlandish schemes stood scant chance of acceptance by the conservative mentality of the practical engineers running military schemes. There was the brilliant Dr Porsche, whose armoured designs ranged from a rejected competitive design for the heavy Tiger tank, to another giant 180 ton machine: and there was another proposal by two men called Grote and Hacker to build a tank weighing over 1,000 tons. Men such as Porsche could enthuse Hitler (who had a strong technical awareness) with the bizarre and by so doing deflect strictly limited research, development, and production facilities from more urgent fundamental projects.

Hitler, convinced that it was due to him that the rot had been stopped in Russia during the 1941 winter panic, took an unhealthy and ever more detailed interest in the shaping of armoured forces in 1942, battening on to the recognised channels of industrial requisitions to promote his schemes. Up to 1942, demands on industry to produce equipment always came as an order from the High Command, each Service fostering certain factories which worked exclusively for them and them alone as a matter of routine – with the result that, at a time when Germany suffered shortage in capacity as well as many items, several factories did not receive sufficient orders to keep them in full employment when their branch of the service had run short of demands. Of course, the tank industry as a whole was never amongst the underemployed but it suffered its fair share of misdirection. For instance, there were confusions over the supply of spares mixed with sudden demands for improvements to old marks of tank at the moment when new ones were being rushed from prototype straight into production. Then there arose feverish concentration on the construction of assault-guns to the detriment of tanks. From lack of effective central direction, the most dreadful confusion permeated the German tank industry in 1942, for while the Wehrmacht ordered tanks and assault guns (and often found its orders varied or reversed by Hitler), industry could only blindly follow each contradictory instruction – always remembering that the SS was a separate agency whose requirements took priority over all others.

Anarchy of this sort could not last indefinitely. Fortunately, in Albert Speer, his Reich Minister for Armaments, Hitler owned the loyalty of a favourite who administered the German industrial complex with a shrewd mixture of good sense, sound decentralisation, and astonishing success, within a national system whose internal workings were being driven into over-centralisation by the megalomania of Hitler. He turned to Speer in 1942 to bring a semblance of order.

Before the débacle at Stalingrad had further stripped the Panzer force of many more tanks, Speer had gone far to deflect industrial control from the Service Ministries, causing the ordering of equipment to pass through his Ministry, instead, by way of a series of Main Committees – of which the principal ones controlled specific major items – while Main Rings controlled materials; and placing the Committees and Rings entirely in the hands of industrialists. Thus, with the exception of the SS, which persistently evaded Speer's control, he had shifted German industry into a position whereby it controlled its own destiny.

After Stalingrad a chastened Hitler seemed momentarily to lose faith in his own military judgement – a change reflected in the freedom enjoyed by Manstein when he won the Battle of Kharkov in his own way. Of more importance to Panzer divisions was Hitler's recall of General Guderian – a complete *volte-face* since Guderian had been disgraced by Hitler (who did not readily forgive) at the end of 1941 and in 1942 had suffered from a heart condition. In February 1943, Hitler made Guderian Inspector-General of Armoured Forces with a Charter of Guderian's devising, the aim of which was to reconstitute the Panzer force which Hitler himself had all but ruined. Hitler gave Guderian complete control over the organisation and training of the armoured forces, including those of the Waffen-SS and

Heavy Armoured Car Sd Kfz 234 series with L/48 75mm gun
Armoured cars were an important part of the reconnaissance component of
Panzer Divisions from their inception. At first they worked alongside motor-cycle
troops and were only lightly armed. Later they acquired much heavier armament,
as with this model, and had to give up all-round traverse. The advantage of armoured
cars over tanks was their silence, greater reliability and range of action. Across
country, however, they were at a severe disadvantage. Weight: 8 tons. Speed:
50mph. Crew: four

the armoured formations that Göring
had managed to turn into a private
army from spare personnel in the
Luftwaffe. Guderian was also em-
powered to lay down the technical
developments and production plans
for weapons in conjunction with
Speer. Thus two men, whose interests
coincided and whose patriotism lay
beyond doubt, met in complete har-
mony to render order where factions
ran wild.

Guderian's main tasks centred on
returning the Panzer force to its
original high state of training and
giving it the weapons which he believed were the real match winners –
tanks. To Guderian's disgust, the
Wehrmacht's Artillery Branch
managed to retain the assault-guns
separate from Panzer forces, preventing him from controlling their evolution at a time when more assault-guns
than tanks were coming from the
factories. Nevertheless he could vary
the proportions of all fighting vehicles
made and issued, even though this
matter had passed almost beyond
rational control. For in a way the
manufacture of assault-guns repre-

sented something more than a
simple means of getting new, more
powerful guns into service quicker
than might have been possible had
that gun needed to wait for a more
complex tank to be prepared for it.
The assault-gun was primarily a
defensive weapon, satisfying Hitler's
fascination for any sort of anti-tank
gun at a time when he intuitively
accepted that Germany had passed
beyond the realisation of further
expansion. If this is so, he omitted to
understand the defensive application
of mobile counter-penetration by
Panzer divisions – but his approach
need not have been quite as illogical
as Guderian and many another German general have suggested.

In any case, Guderian held immense
personal power: not only could he
shape the Panzer force upon which
Germany's future safety depended –
he had direct access to Hitler, and
with that a chance of deflecting more
than matters of tank policy. He could
educate Hitler in the wider military
application of technical affairs, such
as the fallacy of putting too much
faith in the destructive powers of

109

panacea defensive measures against armour. For instance, hollow-charge artillery shells and short-range infantry anti-tank rockets, like *Panzerfaust*, appealed to Hitler, and many others, for being cheap, easily manufactured, and capable of blasting through the thickest armour by chemical instead of kinetic energy. Hitler had to be taught the snags that gave this weapon only a complementary place amongst all the other weapons, yet in grasping at the panacea weapon he merely echoed the timeless thoughts of all those who receive each new anti-tank weapon as the final executioner of the whole tank idea – a tendency which persists to this day.

Amongst the plethora of decisions awaiting Guderian was that concerning which tanks should go on being built. Mark III had gone out of production in late 1942, its chassis becoming a prime mover for assault-guns. There was a proposal for a new light tank, but this too had to be dropped in face of the endless demand for unlimited medium and heavy tanks. Tiger had been sent prematurely into

action and in small number (a typical German User Trial on active service on the Leningrad front, in September 1942, and in Tunisia. In Russia their debut across soft ground had terminated when several bogged and had to be left behind for leisurely examination by Russian experts: the same post-mortem awaited those abandoned after the collapse in Tunisia.

Tiger's rushed entry into service merged with a host of technical unreliabilities as well as a suspicion that its bulk made it cumbersome and a tactical anomaly. Not for nothing did the crews call it 'the furniture van'. Panther was also being hastened into action with such hideous subsequent results that those of the original 325 which could be recovered had to be withdrawn to the Fatherland for rebuilding due to major defects, particularly in the optical, automotive, and steering equipment. The state of confusion that hazed German tank circles can be gathered when it is recalled that a serious proposal to stop production of Mark IV (the one really battleworthy tank still in

Second best – assault guns in production

roduction) before Panther had gone nto action, remained under discussion until finally rescinded in May 1943.

Nevertheless, the acute tank shortage, re-emphasised by the winter losses, finally forced Guderian to accede to a step that went absolutely contrary to his convictions – the temporary substitution of assaultguns for tanks within some Panzer divisions. Had this not been done, the armoured content would have fallen to an all-time low, made all the worse, in Guderian's eyes, when he reflected that officially each Panzer division now only possessed two Panzer battalions each of 48 tanks at the best. Much had gone awry since the palmy days when Guderian's initial establishments demanded 561 tanks. Assault-guns with their limited traverse imposed tactical restrictions on Panzer divisional leaders. During an advance (and Panzer divisions rarely fought except aggressively) a gun without all-round traverse could not deal with the sort of unexpected situation that arose in the forefront of the battle: therefore assault-guns could only be allowed to travel in the rearward echelons to give supporting fire to the tanks in the lead. Thus tanks became even more precious – only one to each thousand men, with the result that there were some who put the rescue of a tank from capture before that of men.

For obvious reasons, the best of the Panzer force was deployed in Russia early in 1943. Of course there were several Panzer divisions scattered throughout Europe from the Balkans through Italy, France, the Low Countries, and Norway, but most of these were low in manpower and feeble in equipment. Some, indeed, were paper divisions, the surviving cadre of some decimated formation that had been wiped out in Russia or Africa but whose existence was being perpetuated by a few old hands while fresh recruits were trained to fill gaping vacancies. Many Panzer divisions such as these could be found in France, learning their trade on old French or Czech vehicles, while chiefly responsible for helping keep order

Testing the run-out of the 75mm gun on a Pz Kw IV

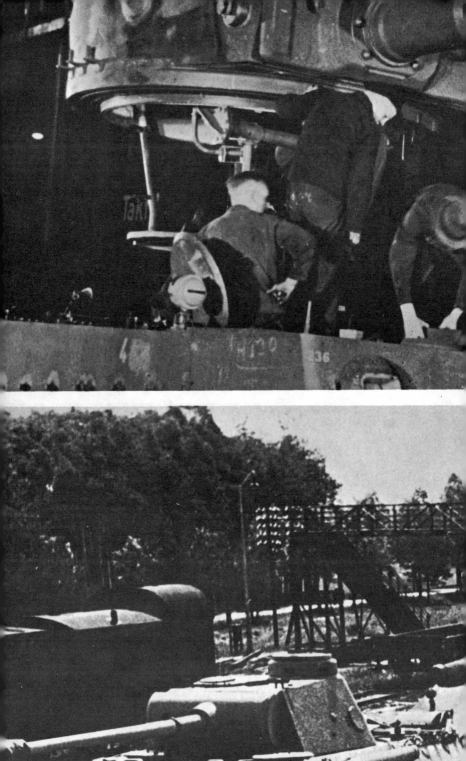

Takt 8

Panther. Railways were nearly always used to move Panzers to the Front.

in territories where the population bore the men no good will. Training most certainly had need to be improved, for even veterans forget basic essentials after prolonged action and nothing falls off quicker than the finer arts of maintenance and gunnery after a long spell in the line.

Yet the principles binding the Panzer force into the tough proposition all its enemies knew never ceased to be those of teamwork, speed, and determination. Constantly the hard-bitten German tank leaders were drumming the need for quick action into the ears of their subordinates. Only by acting promptly, seizing fleeting opportunities, timing each attack with perfect precision to supporting fire and the reaction of the enemy had they repeatedly overcome vastly superior numbers in the past. Now, with the enemy outnumbering them more at every encounter, the Panzer divisions had need to make even better use of their dwindling number of tanks – and somehow had to make up for technical deficiencies as well. For the servicing arrangements still fell short of an acceptable stand-

Panther
This tank was designed as the replacement for Pz Kw III and IV in order that the Panzer divisions could achieve superiority over the Russian T34/76 and parity, at least, with the next generations of allied tanks. The new L/70 75mm gun fired shot at a muzzle velocity of 3,068 feet per second. Weight: 45 tons. Speed: 29mph. Crew: five. 1 x 75mm gun, 2 x 7.9mm machine gun

ard, even when spares could be obtained. Six weeks' training of fitters was not enough and the crews themselves did not always help the fitters as much as they might. In fact it was noted that once the fitters came to a job, the crews hung around and interfered with the work in hand: for all their 'prowess' the tank crewmen exhibited human tendencies at least.

This is not to say that the main body of the Panzer force was by any means spent. Its losses had been serious but not crippling. Many of the surviving originals were desperately tired but still full of fight and able to pass their unrivalled knowledge to the new men drafted in. The trouble was finding sufficient time to train at all, since only rarely could the Panzer divisions be withdrawn for long from the front. Indeed, from 1943 onwards a dilution of the best trained men had to take place in the light of a growing threat of Anglo-American invasion in either Southern or Western Europe.

Fundamentally, however, Guderians' inspiring leadership and cool yet fierce direction had only to give further impetus to an already desperate, almost mystical dedication within the Panzer force and every fighting element of the Wehrmacht. These were badly frightened, worried men who had been closest of all to the terror that 'wild Russian hordes' could engender; but once men with a deeply ingrained fighting skill and spirit, who are frightened, find themselves with their backs against the walls of their own homes, they fight as a warrior sect apart. Thus, when the American President Roosevelt let slip the policy of Unconditional Surrender at Casablanca in January 1943, he gave a fillip to the Panzer soldiers such as Guderian could never have imparted.

Within a few months, Guderian did much to restore order where very little had existed before his return. He then dreamed of the revitalised Panzer force returning to battle and using its improved armaments along with superior accompanying infantry (now entitled Panzer Grenadiers for prestige), in the time honoured method, to trounce all contenders. He knew it could only be German quality versus Allied quantity but he honestly believed that quality, if handled with established principles, could lead Germany to final victory. That was the eternal spirit driving the Panzer force.

The rot sets in

Of the principles most frequently extolled by German tank leaders (and those of other nations too) that of surprise – hand-maid of the unexpected – comes highest on the list. In war, fear can best be disciplined by teaching men how to cope with every conceivable circumstance in an effort to obviate the unexpected: therefore, a good way for an enemy to upset that training is by stimulating the unexpected along with uncertainty. Men hate the unknown.

During the spring thaw in 1943, when the Panzer divisions enjoyed their first respite for ten months, they employed the time re-equipping, absorbing reinforcements, and retraining from grass-roots level. New section and troop training, making the maximum use of live firing (as had always been German practice), took place on every possible occasion. From Speer's redoubled production programme, more tanks began to appear, achieving a real improvement in vehicle strengths, enhanced by the sight of the powerful Tigers, over 300 Panthers and nearly 90 of the so-called Porsche Tigers (sometimes called Ferdinands or Elephants). With them grew renewed confidence in the reviving Panzer force. Notwithstanding the known defects in the Panther and the fact that Ferdinand with its own 88mm gun and single machine-gun (both with very limited traverse) seemed of doubtful combat value, the Panzer divisions possessed greater inherent strength by the end of June 1943 than at any time in their history.

The problem arose, what to do with them? Clearly the massive Russian tank-building industry had replaced the previous winter's losses with new, tougher models ready to be flung into the next battle in greater numbers than ever. Prudence suggested that the German Panzer force should await that assault in order to make full use of the advantages granted by being on the defensive. But Hitler and the German High Command plumped for a spoiling attack, Operation 'Citadel', the pinching out of the Kursk Salient which Manstein had reckoned feasible in April but which, by July, could only be military suicide. As early as May

The Tiger hunts its prey. A T34 burns

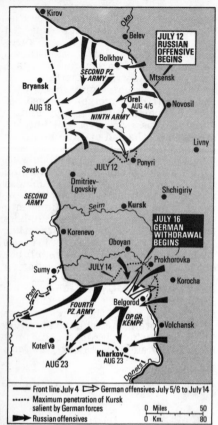

Map 1 (left) labels:
Kirov, Belev, Bolkhov, Bryansk, Mtsensk, Orel AUG 4/5, Novosil, Livny, AUG 18, SECOND PZ. ARMY, NINTH ARMY, Sevsk, JULY 12, Ponyri, Dmitriev-Lgovskiy, Shchigiriy, SECOND ARMY, Seim, Kursk, Korenevo, Oboyan, Prokhorovka, JULY 14, Sumy, Korocha, Belgorod, FOURTH PZ. ARMY, OP. GR. KEMPF, Volchansk, Kotel'va, Kharkov AUG 23, AUG 23, Donets

JULY 12 RUSSIAN OFFENSIVE BEGINS
JULY 16 GERMAN WITHDRAWAL BEGINS

Front line July 4   German offensives July 5/6 to July 14
Maximum penetration of Kursk salient by German forces
Russian offensives
0 Miles 50 / 0 Km. 80

Map 2 (right) labels:
L. Ladoga, Leningrad, ESTONIA, L. Peipus, LATVIA, Kalinin, LITH., Dvina, Moscow, Vitebsk, Vyazma, Smolensk, Minsk, Bryansk, Orel, POLAND, Pripet, Dnieper, RUSSIA, Marshes, Kursk, Voronezh, Zhitomir, Kiev, Kharkov, Poltava, Tarnopol, Donets, Bug, Dnepropetrovsk, Rostov, Odessa, Kerch, CRIMEA, RUMANIA, Danube, Sebastopol, BLACK SEA

0 Miles 200 / 0 Kilometres 400

Front line July 1, 1943
" " Dec 23, 1943
" " June 1944
Russian attacks

the Russians foresaw how tempting
the salient must appear to German
eyes, and in June it became obvious to
the Germans that the Russians had
fortified the bulge in an unprecedented
manner. Yet, on 4th July, Operation
'Citadel' began, backed by no less than
three Panzer divisions against the
northern face of the salient and eight
against the southern, with others in
reserve. Thus did the Germans spurn
strategic surprise by doing the very
thing their enemy expected.

What transpired reads like the
account of any ordinary infantry
assault in the First World War. The
mixed battle-groups rolled forward in
waves against fortified lines and defended localities set amongst numerous villages and copses. Despite
intense German bombing and artillery
preparation, Russian artillery and
machine-gun fire broke out and drove
the German infantry to ground, while
anti-tank gunners picked off the isolated tanks as they strove to come to

grips with the closely knit Russian
fortified positions. Such progress as
was registered gained only a few miles
in an advance that dissolved into a
series of deliberate, head-on assaults
against individual copses and villages.
Gone were the thrilling sweeps of
earlier offensives, for each attack
shunned a tactical as well as a strategic indirect approach, threw surprise
to the winds, and headed exactly
where the Russians hoped they would.
At once the Panthers exhibited the
full set of teething faults they were
known to possess. And when the
Ferdinands broke through the defences, their thick armour giving
them full immunity to fire, they soon
found themselves isolated and hunted
to death because, while no other tanks
or infantry could stay with them, their
solitary machine-gun gave woefully
insufficient local protection. Only a
tiny penetration was made in the
north with a not much bigger one in
the south, and both were contained at

each stage by fierce Russian tank counterattacks from the flanks. By 14th July many Russian tanks had been killed and a great many prisoners taken, but the German Panzer force had been fought to a standstill and drained of its best material.

And this time no opportunity was given to recover, for at the very height of the German effort the Russians opened their own summer offensive and swept forward massively on a wide front lapping either side of the Kursk Salient, recapturing Kharkov, taking Orel, and gradually extending the scope of their activities until practically the entire Eastern Front came ablaze. Faced by odds of four or more to one, and the Russian habit of throwing men and material continuously against a selected point until either they had nothing left to send or had actually broken through, the German Army reverted to the tactics that had saved them after Stalingrad. That is, they gave ground, tried to lure the Russians into traps and struck back hard when momentum seemed to have been lost. This worked satisfactorily for the Germans providing they could maintain their strength in retreat, and so long as Hitler and the High Command gave them a free hand. But, needless to say, that ideal solution was rarely enjoyed. To begin with, the collapse in North Africa had exposed Europe's southern shores to invasion and made it essential to send reinforcements to the Mediterranean, though the mountainous terrains in both Italy and Greece were amongst the last places in Europe where Panzer divisions could find the best employment. Then, as the situation worsened Hitler persisted in throwing out volleys of 'no withdrawal' edicts that imposed immobility on commanders who were imbued with the maxim that it is folly to stand still in an armoured battle.

Never did this maxim seem more important as the Russians improved their tactics, even down to the lower company levels, and when they introduced into service the yet more powerful T 34/85 tank (with an excellent high-velocity 85mm gun) along with the KV-85 carrying a similar gun. More than ever the Germans found that their Tigers and Panthers had to open fire at long range in order to hold the enemy off, but at the same time they had to avoid being taken in flank since the 85 could penetrate their side armour at those same long ranges. Thus the need to move fast from one concealed position to another was mandatory – the more so as Russian aircraft stepped-up their attacks on individual tanks, although with indifferent results.

The Panzer formations had also to keep on the move, because the enemy offensives stretched the length of the battle front, and they, the mobile reserve, needed to be stationed at each threatened place but could not be everywhere at once. Constantly the Germans resisted the temptation to guard too many vital places at once in desperate efforts to conserve the essential mobile reserves. It became, in fact, an interminable struggle to curb Hitler's desire to counterattack every incursion all up and down the line, regardless of the knowledge that inadequate local assaults lost more heavily and achieved less than stronger, better prepared counteroffensives.

By the end of September 1943 the Russian front lay roughly along a line drawn from the west of Leningrad, through Kiev and thence down the course of the River Dneipr to the Black Sea. But the Russian front could no longer be considered separately from Germany's other commitments. For Sicily had been lost by the early part of August, Italy had been invaded and had defaulted from Germany's side in September, and the Anglo-American Armies were creeping close to Rome. Simultaneously the bombing offensive against the Fatherland, which had begun as far back as 1940, but had only grown more than a nuisance in mid-1942, now crushed one German city after another, and in October succeeded in knocking out a number of key tank factories, notably some building Panthers. Each new threat helped dilute the German defences; each front had to be severely rationed. And though Speer's organisation actually continued to raise tank and aircraft production it did not always do so in the most logical manner or with durable quality – particularly when the need to dis-

The assault gun, left, and its victim, a T34, right

perse industry to safer places made quality control yet more difficult to implement.

Newer and even more powerful fighting vehicles kept being designed. That October, Hitler and Guderian viewed mock-ups and prototypes of the next generation of Tiger – Tiger II, sometimes known as 'Royal' or 'King Tiger' – along with the tank-hunting versions of Panther and Tiger ('Jagdpanther' armed with an 88mm gun and 'Jagdtiger' with a great 128mm gun and protected by immensely thick armour). German tank production in 1943 amounted to 5,996 tanks (including 3,073 of the Mark IVs), 3,411 assault-guns and 2,657 self-propelled gun carriages – and still the armoured strength of the Panzer and infantry divisions stuck obstinately below establishment. Losses at the front mounted mostly in step with the fierce intensity of the fighting, and partly as the penalty for piecemeal tactics. But the most serious underlying cause of high losses was the declining standard of training amongst the crews. Gradually that tired prime élite which had won victory in the first three years,

survived the first setbacks, and been stiffened again before 'Citadel', was cracking and being eroded. Its place could not be filled by the uninitiated, many of whom did not live long enough to find out enough about what went on.

Parallel defects afflicted the Luftwaffe – the Panzer divisions' well-tried partner in every successful foray. Up to 1942, help of all kinds had been provided by the airmen whose techniques and close co-operation matured from constant practice. Now the Luftwaffe fought against universally hopeless odds, flying in aircraft that barely matched those of its opponents. Furthermore, first priority had to be given to shielding the Fatherland from the air attacks that threatened the entire German nation. Thus the armies at the front became the first to feel cuts in air assistance, and this deprived the Panzer divisions of reconnaissance and bomber support, as well as the protection afforded by fighter aircraft. From 1943 onwards the Panzer divisions had to move more by night, to learn to conceal themselves more thoroughly from air attack, and to make greater use of artillery in attack and defence. Enemy air attacks of all kinds interrupted supply routes and destroyed supply lorries, while repeated direct attacks on the tanks themselves by low-flying aircraft armed with cannons, rockets, and bombs gave the crews little rest. Direct hits from the air were comparatively infrequent, but even near misses could cause sufficient minor damage to immobilise a tank, and these threw an extra strain on the already overloaded repair teams.

In 1943, therefore, the Panzer force took delivery of its first specialist anti-aircraft tanks in an endeavour to give armoured formations a degree of close protection against low-flying aircraft when deprived of protection from the heavier anti-aircraft guns and the Luftwaffe. Nevertheless, the mounting air threat, which was never as acute in the East as in the West, heaped complications on armoured warfare but failed to bring armour to a halt.

As the result of the policy of deliberate wholesale destruction carried out by the German army as it retreated through Russia, the battles of 1943 and 1944 took place in a wilderness, though not raising the same problems manifest in Rommel's desert campaign: Rommel never had to concern himself about crossing rivers. In Russia, during the German invasion, rivers only caused token pauses since it was rare for the defenders to be able to cover every potential crossing place at once, but in retreat the Panzer divisions looked on rivers as a mixed blessing. Although the High Command treated rivers as strong defensive barriers between the rest of the army and the Russians, the men of the Panzer divisions guessed (usually correctly) whose job it would be to hold open crossing places while the rest of the army struggled through, knowing that they might be last over, making a dash for it with the enemy hard on their heels, hoping to cross the last bridge before it was blown up in their faces.

Not unnaturally, the Russians were no less adept at crossing rivers than the Germans – and far more inclined to waste a few hundred lives in each attempt. In fact, the Russians crossed the Dneipr on 27th September. the same day as the Germans retired to its west bank and, despite a counterattack by a Panzer and a Panzer Grenadier Division (the modern name for the old motorised infantry division), hung on to their lodgement. So the Dneipr never imposed a lasting barrier, even though it was over 400 yards wide, and the Russians showed particular skill in bridging it underwater to enable men to wade across almost unobserved. Thus the battle which the Germans had intended to fight close to the river bank got out of hand from the beginning, failing to circumvent the tank attacks that led to the customary mobile melée breaking out again on the west bank in the middle of October. The Panzer divisions were quite powerless to eliminate the many dozen bridgeheads that mushroomed and then linked up until, for all practical purposes, the entire river line had fallen into Russian hands.

The problems facing the Panzer divisions had taken on new and greater dimensions than before. Because the Russians made so many major advances in such strength, thrusting deeply with strong forces in extended line, it became extremely difficult to locate the true enemy flank against which to project a full-blown envelopment of an entire moving horde. Cutting off Russian spearheads by raiding their supply lines also suffered frequent disappointment – a highly experienced Panzer divisional leader, General von Manteuffel, commented that he had often led raids of that sort and found nothing to attack in the enemy rear other than signal centres. In a way the campaign began to assume the character of mechanised guerilla warfare on a grand scale. Once an offensive had started, each side tried to hold firm bases against the other, and only gave way when the countryside for miles around had become so infested by the enemy that further local domination became pointless. Panzer divisions took to raiding from hides behind the front, debouching upon the Russian rear when a suitable target had been detected. Tank ambushes were the order of the day. Of course, tactics of this type are most fruitfully employed in territory where the civilians are

Jagdpanzer IV
The hunting SP version of Pz Kw IV, this vehicle found extensive employment from 1944 in support of both Panzer and Infantry Divisions. Models with both the L/48 and L/70 75mm gun were produced. The model shown here mounts the latter weapon – the same gun, in fact, as mounted in the turret of the Panther tank. Weight: 24 tons. Speed: 25mph. Crew: five

friendly, and though there were many dissident Russians friendly to the Germans, this was far from a universal tendency.

In the late autumn, when the mud once again stifled movement, the front stabilised temporarily, leaving great gaps yawning wide open between the warring sides. Kiev had fallen soon after the Dneipr had been crossed, though a sharp Panzer battle to the west, in the vicinity of Zhitomir, had cost the Russians dear and stopped them for the moment. With so large a proportion of the Panzer force drawn into action on the Southern Front, the number of armoured vehicles on the Northern Fronts had fallen to only 500 (many of them assault-guns) to be set against the 1,400 Russian machines that struggled west from Vyazma to Smolensk in eight weeks' uninterrupted fighting. In the close wooded country that masked the approaches to Smolensk, the Germans made the Russians pay a high price for each advance such as they, the Germans, had never paid when moving through the same area in 1941. Perhaps best of all, this measures the discrepancy of

skill that gave the Germans a chance against the Russians in 1943. Grossly outnumbered, the Germans still demonstrated how much more vulnerable armoured vehicles had become to improved anti-tank weapons in close country. Here assault-guns came into their own, backing away in company with their infantry and making use of every bit of cover, of minefields, and the rides through the forests where Panzer divisions with their massed tanks were out of place except as a last-ditch reserve. And here, incidentally, where the Russians never made a complete breach of the German line, they too found no opportunity to commit their tank divisions, since the conditions for exploitation never appeared.

The Smolensk affair led to the end of the siege of Leningrad. On this front, too, Panzer divisions were only sparingly used amongst the forest and lakes where assault-guns did even better work than on the Central front. The line drifted back west at the price of heavy casualties to the Russians, for even if they had learnt a lot about armoured warfare since 1941, the

1. Assault gun commander
2. Supply – ammunition for a Tiger
3. SP Artillery support
4. Anti-tank gun support
5. The pity of war
6. Death of a Panzer
7. Supply – petrol for an assault gun
8. Repair – the interminable battle
   with tracks

Germans had learnt still more about winter war, such as how to keep tracked and wheeled vehicles moving on snow, and how to stay alive and go on fighting when the thermometer registered at the bottom of the scale.

To all intents and purposes the battle of the Eastern Front hardly paused throughout 1943 or in the early part of 1944, and that meant that Panzer divisions were constantly at full stretch. It also meant that great quantities of fuel were being consumed when Germany's oil stocks were under air attack and sinking in volume. In Italy a grim battle, in which armour played a secondary role to infantry and artillery, amongst steep mountains and swift rivers, relegated a minimal Panzer strength of one or two divisions to reserve. But all eyes now began to turn to France and the Low Countries because there the next Allied blow could be expected. Guderian seemed to spend more time than ever exploring means to build up armoured strength in the West. With good reason he mistrusted the so-called invulnerability of the Atlantic Wall, knowing that, once the Allies were ashore, an armoured battle must be in immediate prospect and the key to the final outcome. Yet where would he find the necessary men and material when the Russians continued to attack and attack again in the east, throwing the Germans out of the Crimea and thrusting a deep salient into Poland almost as far as Brest Litovsk?

This is the time to assess the state of the Panzer divisions themselves as they squared up to their stiffest tests. From inception, the gradual erosion of their tank strength had been continual, and now that a bare 103 tanks were to be found in the ordinary Wehrmacht Panzer division, the process had reached its nadir. However, there had been compensating increases, not just in the improvement in fighting power of the more modern tanks, but also acquired by the greater mobility inherent in the extra armoured vehicles with better cross-country performance that populated nearly every unit (other than the Panzer regiment) within the division. The Reconnaissance Battalion had shed most of its motor-cycles and been given more heavy weapons, such as armoured assault-guns, to help it fight for information – in the upshot this unit often found itself holding the line when no other unit could be spared. The two Panzer Grenadier regiments now transported half their strength in armoured half-tracks and the remainder in trucks (allowing them to enter the heat of the battle and to fight, if necessary, from their vehicles) and also had a few self-propelled howitzers organic to themselves: while the artillery was also half self-propelled and half motor drawn and containing no less than 18 medium guns of 150mm calibre – an important acquisition in substitution for reduced air support. Half the anti-tank guns were self-propelled and half motor-drawn, and in a few divisions an additional company of assault-guns might still be found, even though Guderian had managed to revert to filling the Panzer regiments almost exclusively with tanks. One outsized Wehrmacht division – Manteuffel's 'Gross Deutschland', owned no fewer than 360 tanks (including 200 Panthers and some Tigers) and 30 assault-guns.

Needless to say the SS Panzer divisions were even better off than most of their army contemporaries, their strengths kept closer to their inflated establishments than the others, with supplementary units, such as a Tiger company, permanently attached instead of allocated as occasion demanded from Army sources. By the same token the SS artillery was both more numerous and of heavier calibre – its six 170mm guns seeming somewhat out of place in a highly mobile formation. But in taking the pick of the manpower available, the SS formations skimmed off the cream that had been the share of the Panzer divisions, and what little of goodness that the latter still received left little or nothing for the rest of the army after the Parachute units had taken their cut. The outcome could only lead to a drastic decline in the quality of the basic infantry formations whose ghastly casualties redoubled for lack of skill linked to poor leadership. During the retreat past Smolensk, the infantry lost the equivalent of a battalion a day – a wastage that drained each front and which could not be recuperated from wholly Germanic manpower. So the infantry divisions became increasingly filled by foreign nationals and men of low grade, and in consequence grew ever less reliable, so that their work had need to be done more and more by the Panzer divisions. Thus, the creation of several competing *corps d'élite* robbed the rest of the army of its essential cadre of leaders and key men with results that were bound to recoil sooner or later. Indeed, in due course, foreign nationals entered the Panzer force, and even certain formations of the Waffen-SS.

Tank production continued to improve throughout 1944, both in quantity and quality. No less than 19,067 armoured fighting vehicles of all sorts (including 3,955 Panthers) were manufactured, and in most the serious weaknesses had been eradicated. The new L71 88mm gun on Tiger II and the 128mm carried in the ungainly Jagdtiger, could match and outmatch, respectively, anything the Russians or Western Allies could produce. Yet this upsurge in gun-power neither solved every battlefield problem nor came about without bringing awkward repercussions in its train. In 1944 General von Manteuffel, when in action against the new Russian Josef Stalin tanks, discovered that his Tigers could not penetrate this enemy tank at 2,000 yards, but had to close to half that distance before making a kill. And since the ammunition for the 128mm gun in Jagdtiger was so bulky and heavy, the charge had to be loaded separately from the shot, thereby reducing the gun's rate of fire.

Each original device and each new bank brought with it extra complexities to add to the time needed for crew training at a moment when time was shortest of all in supply. As a result, full use was not always made of the new devices when the overall standard of basic training was sinking, both technically and tactically. Of course, the decline was gradual and almost imperceptible, while the direction of Panzer divisions by senior commanders and expert staffs, even when hampered by unimaginative strategic instructions, continued with the same fanatical inspiration as before. Since no formation was ever likely to have more than 75% of its tanks on the road at once, a normal Panzer division

Panzer Division leader – von Manteuffel of "Grossdeutschland"

could rarely field more than 80 at a time. Nevertheless, not often would those few tanks be split across a broad front: like wolves they fought in packs, never more dangerous than when cornered and desperate.

Desperation generated fresh fire in the crews as the battle front receded closer to Germany. In Russia the crews had been impressed by the robot-like, blundering, fatalistic massed attacks perpetrated by the enemy soldiers – both mounted and on foot, and so impressed were some German leaders by this inexorable steamroller spirit, that they sought to inculcate it in the German soldiers – with only varying degrees of acceptance. For the fact remained that the Germans retained a clear impression of the main issue at stake – that of sheer survival – and many from the depths of defeat despised the unimaginative Russian lower orders of command until the end, conceding that sheer weight of numbers alone turned the scale in the Russian favour.

However, those Germans who fought only in Russia had no conception of the effects of preponderant air power, as practiced by the Anglo-Americans. Rommel knew – for he had found out in North Africa and witnessed it again in Italy. Now he waited at Rundstedt's side to see how much worse might be the cataclysmic effects of bombing when directed against the Atlantic Wall and the Panzer divisions waiting anxiously in attendance.

Shoring up
the west wall

The German Commander in Chief West, Field-Marshal von Rundstedt, had two fundamental conflicting problems to resolve in the summer of 1944. First he had to prevent the Allies getting through the Atlantic Wall where it guarded the coast from France to Holland – a task that he viewed with cynical detachment in the belief that the war was lost and that the West Wall was a charade. The second problem demanded the metamorphosis of his mobile strategy (based on Panzer Group West, a central reserve of Panzer divisions held ready for concentrated use against each Allied landing), in conflict with the habitual interference to be expected from Hitler and the scepticism of the Commander of his Army Group 'B' – Field-Marshal Erwin Rommel. For the latter, much as he respected Rundstedt and believed in the inherent power of massed armoured formations to strike decisive blows, no longer accepted the feasibility of German armoured formations moving with unrestricted freedom to a distant battlefield in the face of Allied air

supremacy. So, while Rundstedt had planned to withhold the Panzer divisions in depth, and use them once the enemy's main effort had been identified, Rommel wished to locate them close to the coast almost as part of the infantry formations stretched along the length of the seaward defences. In fact, Rommel desired to repeat his Alamein tactics by seeking to destroy the enemy in the frontal defences (on the coast in this case), using the Panzer divisions immediately to prevent the slightest footing being achieved by the enemy. With this in mind he thickened the somewhat hotch-potch shore defences, adding a profusion of minebelts and barriers to the existing system of pillboxes and anti-tank ditches.

A compromise settled the final deployment of the Panzer divisions – Rundstedt giving up his central reserve by permitting Rommel to spread the armour evenly along the coast (but some miles inland), with three Panzer divisions west and four to the east of the River Seine, leaving three in Southern France under the

Armours rival – concrete

ENGLISH CHANNEL

AMERICANS
BRITISH & CANADIANS

Cherbourg
Le Havre
St Lô
Caen
Caumont
Falaise
Vire
Avranches
Argentan
Mortain
Alencon
To Brittany
Rennes
To R.Seine
To R.Loire
Le Mans

Allied thrusts
German pocket Aug 16/19
Miles 0 — 50
Kilometres 0 — 80

Main positions of Panzer Divs after Allied landings
German counterattack Aug 7
Front line August 16

command of Army Group 'G'. Most Germans expected the invasion to come in the Pas de Calais, projecting its main effort along the shortest route to the industrial Ruhr across the superb tank country where the Panzer divisions had won their great triumph in 1940. The possibility of the attack falling on Normandy had been foreseen, but the thick hedgerows and small fields of the *bocage* that characterised that part of France was considered poor tank country – not the sort of territory to which the enemy would wish to commit his armour, and certainly not where the Germans wanted to employ Panzer divisions. These the Germans kept in the open country south and east of Caen.

Rommel reasoned that all previous Allied landings had been led by infantry after a heavy aerial and naval bombardment and therefore enemy tanks would probably not come ashore until the infantry had consolidated a bridgehead: hence it was conceivable that, if the German armour could destroy the invader's infantry bridgehead in time to forestall consolidation, the need to combat the succeeding flood of tanks might be averted. For Rommel wished to avoid tank versus tank engagements, even though his tanks were technically superior. Better than most German Generals he

understood the significance of the Allies' overbearing weight in material.

Rommel was doomed to disappointment, for on 6th June, 1944, after the customary bombardment, Anglo-American armour of a special kind led the assault and systematically set about the destruction of the beach defences at speed before the infantry landed. Swimming tanks came ashore first, followed by wading tanks that flailed paths through the minefields, bridged gaps, filled in tank ditches, and then carried the attack rapidly inland. Closest to the most successful Allied incursion, 21st Panzer Division lay about Caen, and though permission for its intervention in the battle could not be obtained from Hitler (who was asleep) and Rommel (who was on leave) it started to move piecemeal towards those places from whence the British seemed to be threatening Caen. But soon the friction of war intervened in the form of conflicting instructions from various headquarters separating 21st Panzer from Hitler, slowing and bifurcating the advance. Even so the possibility of striking through to the coast only finally came to naught due to the advancing battle-groups being distracted by fresh glider-borne landings taking place on their flank.

By the end of 6th June the Anglo-Americans had defeated Rommel's scheme. They had established bridge-heads and penetrated far enough inland with a mass of armour to give them a margin of safety against almost any attack the Panzer divisions might devise.

Rommel's worst fears were being realised. Sabotage and, above all, massive aerial interdiction of every kind of route, had almost isolated the battlefield from the rest of Europe. Movement by daylight came close to suicide while by night the supply columns found difficulty getting through to the front. The three Panzer divisions west of the Seine came into action fairly rapidly, once Hitler permitted them to do so, but the others were held back in reserve on the assumption that the Normandy landing was a decoy and the main effort to be expected elsewhere. Subsequent orders to send reinforcements to Normandy fell short in execution

A Tiger killed near Falaise

A Panther's feast at Villers-Bocage

because movement could only take place during the short summer nights, and then as a tortuous procession around the miriad detours enforced by broken bridges and blocked roads.

But to return to the days immediately succeeding 6th June. The 21st Panzer Division became involved almost at once in close defensive fighting since they were practically the only troops capable of saving Caen: much of the infantry had been destroyed on the coast, and replacements could only come across the Seine from the Pas de Calais. The 12th SS Division ('Hitler Jugend') arrived in quick time but ran out of fuel, while Panzer Lehr (a very much enlarged division formed out of demonstration units from within Germany, with almost all its Grenadiers carried in armoured half-tracks) did not arrive until the 9th. Not until 10th June could an adequate striking force be concentrated south of Caen – and even then it had constantly to detach elements to cement the front as cracks appeared after continual Allied attacks. The German counter-blow was placed under Panzer Group West whose commander, General Geyr von Schweppenburg, drew his experience from the Russian front where air power played an important but not dominating role. Not only did he fail to camouflage his headquarters, but he and his staff frequently strolled out in their resplendent uniforms to watch Allied bombers doing their work – in fact, right up to the moment they discovered that they had become the target themselves. The subsequent attacks almost wiped out the HQ: worse it completely took the fizz out of Rommel's counteroffensive.

Thereafter the Panzer divisions reached Normandy one by one and bit by bit from all over Europe; and one by one they had to be flung in to hold the line – even amongst the thick of the dreaded *bocage* where a short-range anti-tank weapon could kill a tank with as much ease as a long-range high velocity gun. Here the little, hand-held, bazooka type infantry anti-tank weapons, armed with a hollow-charge warhead, took their toll of tanks from both sides. Here, too, assault-guns could defend as effectively as they had near Smolensk

Jagdpanther
This is the tank hunting version of the Panther tank equipped with an L/71 88mm gun with a traverse limited to 13° either way. With 80mm of sloped frontal armour, this was a formidable fighting vehicle, though suffering from the usual limitations associated with all SP guns when compared with tanks. Weight: 51 tons. Speed: 29 mph. Crew: five. When firing APCBC ammunition at 1,000 yards the 88mm gun would penetrate 170mm armour plate sloped at 30°

and Leningrad, and here mines hampered the operations of each side in nearly two months' savage close combat. Throughout, the Allies managed to build up their forces at a greater rate than the Germans, but in the *bocage*, where the close packed contestants rarely presented a vulnerable front to each other, each attack became head-on, the defence held sway and the greater firepower and superior armour of the German armoured vehicles gave them more than an edge in every encounter with their opposite numbers. The Allies' Sherman tanks, even when armed with an American 76mm gun, were no match for Panthers and Tigers: the British modified Sherman with a 17-pounder gun alone approached the penetrative power of the German 75mm and 88mm guns. In numbers alone were the Allies superior, though in bravery and individual skill there was little to choose between the soldiers of two dogged opponents.

Tactical rules dictated that the main armoured battles should take place in the open country south of Caen, and since those rules made it mandatory for a Panzer divisional

commander to foresee and plan against all eventualities, the Germans foresaw and rehearsed appropriate counteractions against any Allied attack towards Falaise. Thus, when the British launched a blow from Caen on 18th July behind a truly awe-inspiring aerial bombardment, the only surprise suffered by the Germans came from the scale of the onslaught. But the fact that the Germans held the front line only lightly caused a considerable proportion of the preliminary attack to waste itself on empty ground. Thereafter, as three British armoured divisions raced towards Falaise through the bombed zone, it was to find themselves pounded at long range by the guns of three Panzer divisions supplemented by an assortment of Tigers and assault-guns that moved smoothly into predetermined hull-down positions on high ground to the south. The slaughter of British tanks eventually passed the 200 mark – those of the Panzer divisions but a small fraction of that in a battle where the German tanks fought at long range without unduly exposing themselves to fire.

For all their technical superiority, the Germans envied the Allies their numbers, and the fact that the Germans could only field assault-guns, to support their infantry formations, when the Allies could afford to use tanks with their greater offensive capability. Much play has been made by pundits of the so-called wasteful manner in which both Americans and British tended to allocate some tanks primarily to infantry support and others to pursuit; in fact the Germans, who are supposed to have eschewed this system, performed it under the guise of assault-gun support – and thereby did so in a somewhat inefficient manner.

Allied strategy, under Generals Eisenhower and Montgomery, sought to lure German armour and then hold it in the vicinity of Caen while the Americans broke out on the west side of the bridgehead from the direction of St Lô. But as we have seen, the Panzer divisions *wanted* to stay close to Caen – they only got involved in the *bocage* on the American front because, once the German infantry formations had been worn down by Anglo-

American attrition, their place had to be taken in the line by Panzer divisions. So when the Americans broke out on 25th July, it was to dispute with a few half-broken infantry divisions and a couple of understrength Panzer divisions fighting in ground that was the opposite of their choosing.

Unhappily for every element of the German Armed Forces, the atmosphere brooding round their higher commanders sapped all traces of confidence. On 20th July an attempt to assassinate Hitler – the celebrated Bomb Plot – collapsed in fiasco. The Battle of Normandy came to a climax against the background of a witch hunt that undermined the judgement of every member of the German General Staff, whether they had been involved with the plotters or not. Rommel had been involved, but he was seriously wounded by an air attack on 17th July and eliminated from the command structure at a critical moment on all counts. From 20th July onwards no single field commander, not even the darlings of the SS, dared resist Hitler's will, for to do so courted

Tiger II
'Royal 'or 'King' Tiger was only occasionally integral with the Panzer Division,
but frequently worked in close co-operation with them. It first made its appearance
in 1944 and was the most powerful fighting vehicle in service in the Second
World War. Weight: 67 tons. Speed: 18 mph. Crew: five. 1 x L/71 88mm gun.
3 x 7.9mm mg.

misinterpretation of loyalty followed
by quick extinction. But already the
leadership in the West had gone
through a complete turnover. Rundstedt had been sacked and Rommel
wounded before the Bomb Plot. Now
Field-Marshal von Kluge filled both
vacancies – but an association with
the plotters left him wide open to
Hitler's retribution, forcing him to
face the battlefield crisis with a sense
of personal doom affecting his every
decision.

As was to be expected, the Americans
had attacked near St. Lo behind a
pulverising carpet of bombs. Un-
luckily for Panzer Lehr, which happened to be holding that portion of the
line, the bomb pattern practically
coincided with its divisional boundaries: so what little of the division
escaped the impact survived in no
condition to contest the remorseless
advance that followed. Fighting raged
across the bridgehead. Where the
Canadians aimed a reciprocal blow
towards Falaise they were repulsed as
efficiently as the British a week before
on the same ground – thus releasing
several Panzer divisions for action

against the American thrust to the
west. By 30th July the slow initial
progress of the Americans accelerated
as they approached Avranches, whence
they could turn west into Britanny or
east into Metropolitan France. Counter blows by two panzer divisions
against the American flanks had been
brushed aside and inflicted hardly a
pause, for the good reason that the
blows constituted an obvious counter
measure against an enemy who was
prepared and not in the least extended.
Thus, the first counter-action failed
for being inescapably premature. On
the 30th, the centre of gravity of the
battle took a further step to the west
when British infantry and armour
chimed in on the American left flank
by attacking close to Caumont in the
direction of Vire – a move that coincided with Kluge's movement of three
Panzer divisions (the 9th and 10th SS
with 21st Panzer) west from Caen to
make one grand effort at amputating
the American arm before it could
reach out from Avranches.

Vire was a route centre and destina-
tion for the assembling trio of panzer
divisions. But the British and Ameri-

cans made such fast progress towards Vire that they interposed between the German thrust and its selected target. Thus, as the front expanded, the three Panzer divisions found themselves diverted to patching a crumbling line instead of executing a full blooded counterstroke.

After 1st August the American drive past Avranches knew no bounds as it turned west into Britanny, south to the River Loire and, of greatest peril to the Germans, around Caen east towards Le Mans. By 2nd August neither rhyme nor reason favoured a German attempt to cut through to Avranches – the American break-through had grown so enormous that it threatened the total envelopment of every German formation in the area. But on that day came the irresistible Hitlerian demand for a massive counterstroke by eight of the nine available Panzer divisions aimed straight at Avranches – and Kluge, terrified for his life, lacked the wit to discover a way to evade what he knew to be strategic suicide.

When mechanised formations, with thousands of vehicles, move in dispersion over wide landscapes, the problems of traffic control – even in face of heavy air attack – need not impose overburdening staff problems, because cross-country movement reduces congestion on the roads. But when numerous Panzer divisions are ordered into a narrow tract of heavily intersected country that wilts under constant aerial bombardment, and is pitted against an enemy who is unshaken and revelling in the full flood of exploitation, the chances of achieving a coherent attack are remote and the probabilities of utter confusion nigh certain. By selecting 6th August as the day for the armoured counter-thrust, Kluge wasted more lee-way than he could afford and yet denied sufficient time to permit the requisite concentration. Of the eight Panzer divisions originally earmarked, only four got into action, made an initial penetration close to Mortain, and were stopped dead by interminable air attacks and the stubborn defiance of American soldiers fighting from within strong natural defensive positions. Every move by daylight drew fire from the sky – the German soldiers disliking

at first, in particular, the rockets launched by British aircraft, but learning, in due course, that these free flight missiles hardly ever scored a direct hit. Nevertheless, near misses were quite sufficient to destroy soft transport, and the severe toll of burning lorries blocking every lane imposed serious restrictions on the deployment of the German battle-groups. By 7th August the counter-blow had floundered, stranding its participants at the end of a limb.

Fight as hard as they might between Caen and Falaise – and the fanatically

skilful resistance of the young lads of 12th SS Panzer Division in that sector throughout the first fortnight of August wrote a saga of its own – the Germans could do nothing to stem the deluge of American armour flooding round their southern flank under the urgent pressure of Lieutenant-General Patton. On 8th August the Panzer divisions lay impotent and exposed at Mortain. Common sense demanded they ought to be pulled right out of Normandy in order to fight a delaying action back to the River Seine and, if need be, to the Somme. But Hitler said 'no', dug in his toes, and left the Germans to shrink into whatever cover they could find amongst the *bocage* to wait for an inevitable obliteration.

Elsewhere disasters of terrible magnitude copied the Normandy debacle. In Italy the retreat past Rome went on, and in Russia gigantic calamities had befallen. The Russians had withheld their summer offensive until June 22nd and then thrown a vast array west from between Mozbyr and Vitebsk, bursting through the German defences to the northern edge of

that followed the events of 20th July, General Guderian found himself elevated to the post of Chief of the General Staff – a fitting climax, on paper, for the man to whom the Panzer force owed so much.

But Guderian's title bore no relation to its previous glory. Hitler held all the cards close to his chest: the Wehrmacht ceased to wield power and the Chief of its General Staff did little more than command the Russian front – impeded by Hitler's veto. Generals of the SS acquired ever greater power – and proved their

Self-propelled artillery near Caen

Bocage

the Pripet marshes, racing for Warsaw and, as they did so, enlarging the breach so that it seemed nothing could ever block the never ending waves of attackers. Inevitably German losses were extremely heavy, particularly amongst formations that got left behind in the rush. Inevitably too, the effects of the Bomb Plot warped strategic and tactical decisions: the petulant prohibition of timely withdrawal led to more and more German morsels being dropped for enemy consumption. And as a byproduct of the reshuffle in command

worth, for they, best of all, merged ability with Hitler's trust and could more easily circumvent his wilder decrees. Thus the day when the Commander of I SS Panzer Corps (Sepp Dietrich) could be denied leadership of a major armoured operation (as ordained by Rundstedt and Rommel, when they preferred to use Schweppenburg's ill-fated HQ Panzer Group West on 10th June in Normandy) had departed for ever. Rough tough men now took over from the smoother leaders of the old school – the presence of the brilliant, thrusting Field-

Allied bombing at its most intense

Pz Kw IV in Holland

British Cromwell shot in the bocage

75mm anti-tank gun hidden in the bocage

Marshal Model (one of Hitler's favourites), to replace the discredited Kluge in France, acting as a sort of counterpoise to the appointment of the angry, bluff Guderian in Russia.

But though both Guderian and Model could work miracles in a minor way and exploit every advantage surrendered by triumphant opponents, they could not hope to evaporate worthwhile portions of their opponent's strength or materialise fresh Panzer divisions to revitalise the Wehrmacht.

With every front in turmoil and shrinking closer to the original German frontier, the option of holding on one and striking against another grew more remote. The several battle fronts had to be considered as a whole – but no reserves could be shifted from one to another in August 1944. In Normandy what little remained of Fifth Panzer Army (the old Panzer Group West) struggled in a pocket, frantically trying to extricate as many of their colleagues as they could. An American jaw closed from the south, and an Anglo-Canadian jaw from the north, until they finally

snapped shut on 19th August. Even as they did so, a second envelopment of more deadly portent loomed along the Seine, for Patton, having seized Paris on the 22nd, now swept up still greater captive hauls as German refugees made a despairing dash in search of safety on the east bank of the river. The Allied victory was almost complete – the price to Germany losses of over 2,000 tanks and assault guns – approximately a sixth of the year's total production.

No Grand Central Armoured Reserve now barred the way to either the Russian thrust against the Baltic States, the centre of Poland, the Rumanian oilfields at Ploesti, the entire southern half of France (where an Allied landing on 15th August was being prospected at full speed up the Rhone Valley), or in Northern France and the Low Countries. So far as France was concerned, it is doubtful if a reserve could have been despatched thence from Germany, even had one existed, since the chaotic state of road, rail and inland water systems were bringing normal civil distribution to a halt – let alone leaving spare capacity for emergency military traffic. Yet patiently, and with astonishing faith, the Germans began to rebuild formidable reserves along her frontiers in the west, where the old Siegfried Line crumbled in mid-dilapidation and, in the east, where the Rivers Vistula and Danube interposed a tenuous shield. The genius of the Germans in retrieving fleeing soldiers, re-equipping them, and binding them together into comprehensive combat units capable of meeting the shock of battle, fighting shoulder to shoulder with unknown comrades, stands pre-eminent amongst their many achievements in the latter part of the Second World War. Uniformity of purpose and training had much to do with it, and nowhere was this stronger than amongst the survivors from Panzer divisions.

Thus, as the Anglo-American pursuit scorched across France into Belgium, cutting off crowds of milling bewildered Germans, it also swept before it a few indomitable parties who laid ambushes in their trail or who hurried into Holland, there to man as many new armoured vehicles as could be delivered, to hold the frontiers of the Reich. Looked at as an exercise in military organisation, the reconstitution of a coherent defence along Germany's eastern and western borders was wholly laudable – though as an exercise in practical strategy it might have seemed laughable were not the example of so many gallant men doing their duty, so splendid – and perhaps pitiful – to behold. Nevertheless, the staunch German defenders could not have prevailed had not both the Anglo-American and Russian Armies been seized in the autumn of 1944 with the disease afflicting all mechanised armies at the end of over-stretched supply lines – petrol shortage. The Russians came to a halt at Warsaw early in August – maintaining that they had not the strength to exploit beyond the Vistula, even to save Polish patriots wrapped in a death struggle with the Germans within the city – and the Anglo-Americans grappled with a fuel crisis within a week of crossing the Seine. Thus a fortuitous stalemate set in across the battered eastern approaches to Germany while Western armies faltered and stopped once they hit the outer German defences and found that, without support from numerous tanks and artillery, their infantry could make no worthwhile progress except at an exorbitant cost in lives.

As had been common in Russia, the German leaders responsible for the western approaches to the Fatherland managed to detect the early signs of Allied exhaustion with as much ease as they perceived the direction of each major Allied thrust line. Model could partly discount those Allied forces that moved east from Paris and made for the Saar Basin through the Belfort Gap; but he could not allow much elbow room to the columns moving towards Cologne and the southern Ruhr past Aachen, and these he tried to hold amongst strong fortifications on the frontier. Indeed, until a great Allied air armada laid a carpet of airborne troops from Eindhoven to Arnhem on 18th September, Model might have been excused for thinkng that the American drive to Aachen represented the main Allied punch. Therefore, it was no fluke that the Allied paratroopers found newly collected armoured reserves where they landed since the landing zones coincided with orthodox assembly areas for a stroke against the American drive to the Ruhr.

Airborne troops are highly vulnerable to every sort of opposition when first they land, and constantly in jeopardy to tanks until they are joined by heavy anti-tank weapons, including friendly tanks or assault guns. The British 1st Airborne Division that landed at Arnhem some 60 miles north of advancing British armour, arrived on the doorstep of both 9th and 10th SS Panzer Divisions. Neither German formation had recovered its strength, yet neither had lost its élan, and the battle to contain the British parachutists dragged them into a furious scrap within the rubbled streets and splintered woods of the Dutch town – where the enclosed nature of the terrain did much to save the British from a much speedier destruction at the hands of the German armoured soldiers than might otherwise have been the case. As it was, the British failed to push armour

Tigers in a French wood

through to Arnhem in time to buttress the parachutists before they had to be withdrawn or overwhelmed. But in fighting this slogging battle the German defenders of Arnhem brought an end to high mobility in the West.

The Allies had need to repair their supply organisation before embarking on the final subjugation of Germany. Above all this implied the reduction of those German garrisons holding the outlying approaches to the port of Antwerp – the key to the rapid creation of massive Allied strength close to the North German Plain.

On the face of it there was little the Germans could offer in the way of a major riposte. Panzer divisions were of no use in the soft wet lands of Holland – and in any case were in no state for extensive operations exposing them in daylight to the mercy of the ever present Allied air contingents. But as winter approached, with its longer nights and poor flying weather, the opportunities for offensive ground action increased, while the strength of the Panzer force rose in quantity if not in quality. No army,

it seemed to Allied Intelligence – not even an élite – could recover from the pummelling the Panzer divisions had sustained on all fronts during 1944, and still mount offensive operations. That they could operate at all seemed a miracle.

Yet attack they did, as the defenders of the road leading to Eindhoven often discovered when German armour raided the supply convoys trundling along it throughout September, and as the 7th US Armoured Division learnt on 27th October when struck by 9th Panzer Division and pushed back near Helmond – a move whose initial success typically and ironically prompted Model to contemplate exploitation in the manner accustomed. These were classic small German actions that disguised the underlying frailty of the western defence line – and indeed the desperate situation in which Germany found herself. For now that the Allied Air Forces took off from the airfields on Germany's doorstep, a constant state of alert and fear hammered industry, inland transport and, above all, morale. Nevertheless her people were kept going by endless promises, fear of the Russians and the Gestapo, and the Micawberish hope of something turning up. Yet men like Speer could not ignore statistics stating that, of 1,764 tanks manufactured in September, October and November, only 1,371 had reached the troops because of transport disruption: they could further reflect that the production figures themselves showed a fall of something like twenty percent.

The time to worry about production however, was long since passed. Even manpower seemed of lesser importance, despite boys, the dregs of the nation, and many skilled industrial workers being drafted into front line units alongside hosts of foreign nationals. In fact, a far more calamitous threat hung over the Wehrmacht and the Luftwaffe. Their very lifeblood – oil and petrol – was fast drying up.

The last reserve

Exhaustion

When an Army finds it possible to advance 450 miles against opposition in five weeks, the time has come to ask if the puny efforts of the opposition are worthy of further consideration. That was the distance gained by the Russian Armies when they surged forward in the summer of 1944, to the gates of Memel on the northern front Warsaw in the centre and Belgrade in the south.

Throughout this headlong retreat the Panzer divisions and other German formations fought with desperate skill and courage, even though the results rarely seemed to justify the sacrifice. By early autumn, when the mud intervened and the Russians had to turn their energies to the reconstruction of communications across the desolate wastes pounded down by the passing battle, the Germans had lost immense tracts of territory – including portions of German soil – and had abandoned vast quantities of material in their train. What matter that for almost every German tank destroyed, as many as five Russian machines might be seen lying battered and burned by its gun? The Russian tank formations were backed by inexhaustible resources and the Germans by less and less. Tanks and assault guns took on the value of the rarest commodity – but even their value fell to zero with no fuel to burn.

In April 1944 Germany's oil stocks stood at about one million tons – much of it drawn from the Rumanian oilfields at Ploesti, the rest from synthetic plants at home. At the end of August barely 327,000 tons remained, the Russians were on the fringes of the Ploesti fields and the Anglo-American bomber offensive had ravaged the synthetic producing plants. In September, shortly before Ploesti fell, the Wehrmacht had its fuel allocation cut by half – of natural resources, only the microscopic Hungarian and home fields remained. At the same time the Germans instituted a thorough comb-out of every possible source of manpower throughout the Fatherland, going so far as to draft skilled factory workers into the armed forces at the expense of weapon production. True, the men thus given

to the services were of high quality, but the time to train them for battle was ludicrously short and the long term effects on industry catastrophic. But Hitler's mania evaded reason, and linked self-immolation to the destruction of his nation.

Yet this freshly discovered manpower bank went far to restock establishments during the short respite granted by the halting of both major Allied offensives at the borders of the Reich. Only in the vicinity of Budapest did the Russians prosecute offensive operations, and here they made only slow and costly progress that drew upon itself an increasing German reaction. All Germany's eastern Allies were deserting her under the pressure of Russian attacks, and so the defence of Budapest devolved upon the Germans when the Hungarians faded out. On other parts of the front new defensive positions were constructed, enabling Panzer divisions to be drawn into a shortlived reserve for refitting. But these reserves were weakening and purely local, divorced from the reconstitution of a powerful central reserve elsewhere.

The flood of newly discovered manpower joined to the residue of tank production, fuelled by the dregs of the oil reserves, found their way into an armoured reserve stationed close to Germany's western fortress line. Deciding that the only possible hope of salvation lay in crippling one or other of the enemies at the door by offensive action, Hitler opted for an attack on the Americans, reasoning that the Russians would be too tough a proposition while the Americans, so he thought, had no heart for the fight and might crumple to the discomfort of their British partners. So Hitler committed Germany's last armoured reserve to a death ride before Christmas in a stroke through the Ardennes, over the River Meuse, past Brussels to Antwerp, to cut off the northern wing of the Allies from their supply base and wreck preparations for a spring offensive. The project was ambitious and entirely dependent on Panzer divisions for any lasting success, linked to the hope that the short winter days and poor visibility would spare the vulnerable columns from the massive air attacks that they must provoke.

To execute the scheme, nine Panzer divisions, four of them SS, all at various strengths and widely different states of proficiency, were lined up from Echternach to Monschau ready to jump off on 15th December. The main blow was to be delivered on the northern sector of the Ardennes by the newly formed Sixth SS Panzer Army under Dietrich: four SS Panzer divisions comprised his main striking force. In the southern sector Manteuffel's Fifth Panzer Army, with three Panzer divisions, prepared for a lesser role. In general reserve waited the remaining two Panzer divisions, while the balance of the force comprising as many Volks and Panzer Grenadier divisions as possible plus an infantry heavy Seventh Army under instructions to force a defensive screen along the south flank of the advancing Fifth Panzer Army.

Throughout the autumn the Panzer divisions were secretly withdrawn from the line, hidden away in the Eifel

The Russian flood reaches the Fatherland

Mine laying

SP Artillery in the snow

Assault gun and passengers

Target — a brewed up T34/85

88 in the dark

Target — a JS2 and its conqueror

and neighbouring countryside, re-equipped and trained for their forth-coming task. The German High Command had lost none of its skill, while the Allies signally failed to interpret evidence of impending events and forecast the murderous blow being prepared. Considering the awful future staring the Germans in the face and the utter hopelessness of their condition, the enthusiasm injected into the men of the Panzer divisions that December bears witness to the most astonishing confidence in their cause and unshaken prowess. A great number seem to have been swept away by the hope that their efforts would deliver a really decisive blow and reverse the ill-fortunes of war in Germany's favour.

Those amongst the Panzer leaders who still believed (and none dared express his disbelief), still could not persuade themselves that they might do more than inflict a temporary delay on the Allies: dreams of reaching Antwerp touched on fantasy – orders from above calling for rapid, ruthless exploitation and the bold bypassing of centres of opposition found the minds of their executants tuned to recent

battles in which the line was held and opposition eliminated as it disclosed itself. A lot of the old zip had left the Panzer divisions and had been re-placed by a strict pragmatism.

Nevertheless, the conditions for attack lay firmly in the German favour when they set off on the 16th. A resounding barrage from over 2,000 guns dazed the few Americans holding the front and took the entire Allied Command by complete surprise: they had got used to fighting on the ad-vance; the defensive was a transient phase; retreat a forgotten art. Fog cloaked the advancing Germans when they fell upon the defenders and pushed urgently westwards: their infantry and Volksgrenadier divisions making the breach, followed by the Panzer divisions. Fifth Panzer Army made excellent progress, pushing on unremittingly all day and into the night by the light of searchlights reflecting their beams from the same low clouds which effectively shielded the columns from the slightest aerial interference by day. Fifth Panzer Army reached most of its objectives, but this Sixth SS Panzer Army failed to do, principally because it had been

147

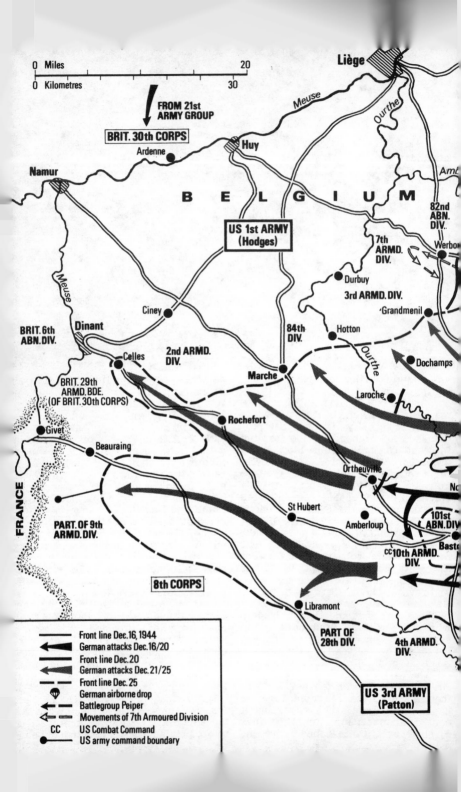

Liège

0 Miles 20
0 Kilometres 30

FROM 21st ARMY GROUP

Meuse

Ourthe

BRIT. 30th CORPS

Ardenne

Huy

Amb

Namur

B E L G I U M

82nd
ABN.
DIV.

US 1st ARMY (Hodges)

7th
ARMD.
DIV.

Werbo

Durbuy

3rd ARMD. DIV.

Meuse

Ciney

Grandmenil

BRIT. 6th ABN. DIV.

Dinant

84th
DIV.

Hotton

Dochamps

Celles

2nd ARMD. DIV.

Ourthe

BRIT. 29th ARMD. BDE. (OF BRIT. 30th CORPS)

Marche

Laroche

Givet

Rochefort

Beauraing

Ortheuville

No

FRANCE

St Hubert

PART. OF 9th ARMD. DIV.

Amberloup

101st
ABN. DIV

CC 10th ARMD. DIV.

Bast

8th CORPS

Libramont

PART OF 28th DIV.

4th ARMD. DIV.

US 3rd ARMY (Patton)

◄━━	Front line Dec. 16, 1944
	German attacks Dec.16/20
═══	Front line Dec. 20
◄▨▨	German attacks Dec.21/25
─ ─	Front line Dec. 25
⬥	German airborne drop
◄━ ─	Battlegroup Peiper
◄▱▱	Movements of 7th Armoured Division
CC	US Combat Command
●	US army command boundary

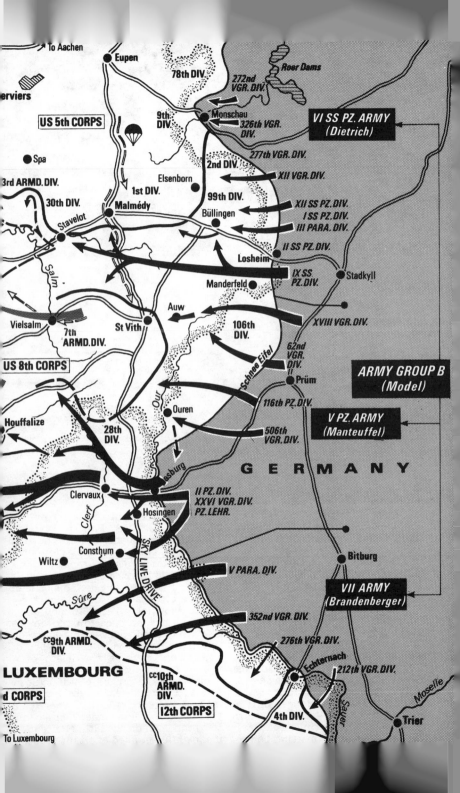

sent against the best defended and most intricate sector in direct contravention of the unimpeachable Panzer maxim that demanded attack on weakness plus the need to avoid complex defended terrain if possible.

Dietrich's Sixth SS Army certainly made penetrations, but not in the right direction or at the requisite pace. In vital sectors there were rebuffs and deflections, and each rebuff led to a pause, each pause to slippage of the programme, each slippage a reduction in the chances of disturbing the Allies' poise and so inducing a collapse and opening the road into the Allied rear. Dietrich advanced only 6 miles the first day while Fifth Panzer travelled nearly three times that far, finding the opposition melting before

it. Dietrich did a little better on the 17th, his 1st SS Panzer Division thrusting on another 14 miles beyond Monschau, but in the thick of mounting resistance the German troops exposed the rawness of their training by tending to engage opposition instead of bypassing it. Moreover, no strict parallel with 1940 could be drawn; on that occasion movement free from traffic congestion had been feasible chiefly due to the absence of opposition; now in the heart of a tough fight, traffic blocks choked every road and prevented the bulk of the SS Panzer divisions even coming into action. Gradually Dietrich's thrust – the crucial endeavour – came to a standstill on the 18th. Manteuffel, meanwhile, enjoyed exultant success.

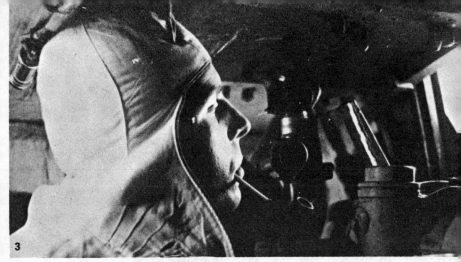

1. Assault gun crew – commander
2. Assault gun crew – gunner and loader
3. Assault gun crew – driver
4. Bogged
5. Tank commander
6. Assault gun with its infantry

On the day Dietrich stalled, Manteuffel surrounded the important route centre of Bastogne, caring not too much for evidence of a vigorous American garrison holding the place, but trusting in the course of events to squeeze the defenders out of their holes when the pressure went on. Meantime, Manteuffel pursued his predetermined course and curled north-westward in the direction of the Meuse crossings at Dinant – where Rommel had won his first success in 1940. Now was the time for Hitler to pocket his pride and peel off SS Panzer divisions from Dietrich to reinforce Manteuffel's success – a permission only grudgingly given since it hurt his political principles in addition to exposing his faulty initial plan.

The outcome could not long be in doubt. Dietrich stuck fast and Manteuffel failed to reach the Meuse for lack of strength due to a supply shortage made worse by the choke blocking his main supply route at Bastogne, where the Americans defiantly declined to surrender. The narrow Ardennes' lanes throttled the Panzer divisions of fuel and circumscribed freedom of manœuvre. On 18th December when Dietrich stopped, both Rundstedt and Model appreciated that the offensive had failed, and later petitioned Hitler to withdraw to the starting point while the sacred central reserve remained intact. But Hitler – predictably – refused to disgorge what had just been won. If there could be no forward movement there certainly would be nothing retrograde. One detects the petulance of a father who, when he has failed to mould his offspring in his own image, revels in inflicting sadistic punishment that simply compounds evil.

In fact the Americans had come close to breaking and for a while the whole Allied command structure had wobbled. But their fighting men had made up for the frailties and miscalculations of their leaders; and when the weather cleared on 23rd December, the air forces descended in swarms upon the hapless Germans exposed in stranded columns on crowded roads and tracks. Fume as he might, Hitler could not push his men further. The offensive dried up, reverted to the defensive, and then turned into a sulky withdrawal as their late prey turned upon them in fury.

On 12th January, while the Central German Armoured Reserve floundered in the Ardennes Salient, the Russians launched their anxiously-awaited winter offensive along practically the length of the front from the Carpathian Mountains to the Baltic. Wherever the Russians struck they did so with overwhelming forces packed in dense formations. No longer could the Panzer divisions try to stem the flood; their every act became motivated by self-preservation and the desire to fight a way out of trap after trap – always in the hope that, perhaps, the nightmare might end, always with disappointment when Hitler continued to goad them to no conceivable purpose. Terror at Russian enslavement kept many fighting in accord with the belief that death would be better than Russian domination.

No Panzer divisions any longer assumed a recognisable shape. Even a few tanks, supported by a miscellany of guns and infantry, might appear on the maps of the High Command invested with the full panoply of its former power, and be ordered to carry out some task far beyond its strength.

By 16th January a multiple threat loomed over Hungary, Silesia, and the North German Plain, including Berlin; and away in the Ardennes the German offensive had been followed by an enforced defensive and some

minor abortive operations in Alsace and Holland. That day Hitler decided to shift Sixth SS Panzer Army to the east – not to guard his capital or counter the main Russian spearheads approaching the River Oder Line, but instead to be sent to Hungary as part of a wild plan to relieve Budapest and attempt to hold on to a few minor oilfields. So while the Panzer reserve went to a front of fading importance, the defences protecting East Prussia, the whole of Poland and Berlin began to disintegrate. Minor penetrations achieved by Sixth SS Panzer Army

Panthers in the Ardennes

upon its arrival in Hungary escaped notice against the clamour surrounding the overall collapse elsewhere and, in due course, even that Army reverted to a desperate defensive with little or no hope of survival.

At the end of January 1945 not a score of feeble Panzer divisions propped up the Eastern Front, while less than half that number wilted under air attack in the west where the daily signs of an approaching major offensive were fulfilled on 8th February when a British attack began to roll up the Siegfried Line, starting west of Cleve and grinding south-east through sodden ground and the dense trees of the Reichswald. Further south the Americans chopped at the remains of the Ardennes Salient and prepared for the moment when they could join the British in crushing the Germans who had been told to defend every inch of German soil west of the River Rhine. Deep flooding along the American front near Roermond prevented the Americans from attacking on time, so with only the British as contenders, and fierce ones at that, the Germans could not withhold reinforcements to the Reichswald to stop

the British breaking out from the confined neck between the Rhine and the Maas. There, almost the last Panzer divisions left in the west went to their doom in an attritional blood and mud bath that was totally foreign to their natural habitat, fighting bitterly to support Parachute Divisions in the spirit of mutual self-sacrifice that typified all German elite formations. By the end of February the last German reserves had been drawn to the north, leaving something like a vacuum for the Americans to enter when they raced north to join the British; there

simply was no German mobile counter force worthy of the name to stop them. Ironically the last Panzer attacks passed, hardly noticed by their opponents.

So in the West, the Panzer divisions died with a sigh. And when the Rhine had been cleared on its western bank and the Americans stole a march by seizing an undemolished bridge at Remagen, all the Germans could send to seal off this surprise crossing of their sacred waterway amounted to scratch infantry units backed by a few assault guns. The armoured defence of Western Germany could no longer be computed in Panzer divisions: now the tally merely comprised individual vehicles. For instance, when Patton's Third Army leapt the Rhine at Oppenheim and Hitler asked if there was no Panzer regiment that could be sent there, he was told that everything was already committed elsewhere but that five Jadgtigers might be despatched from workshops at Sennelager within the next day or so, when, in fact, the cherished five were already earmarked to go to Remagen.

Montgomery crossed the Rhine into the North German Plain on 24th March with such overwhelming Anglo-American forces that the puny German screen waiting to receive them might have felt highly flattered, had they the time to consider the matter. Naturally the flood of armour that soon flowed across the famous river could do as it liked – there were no Panzer divisions to stop it, only a hotch-potch of scattered groups, some fighting frantically to the death, but most only too willing to surrender. Soon the industrial Ruhr, from which so much of the hardware to equip the Panzer divisions had come, had been invested and snuffed out of the reckoning.

Then from the east came the Russians with their final armoured drive to Berlin beginning on 16th April with a breach of the Oder Line. By the 21st the front cut Berlin's suburbs and Anglo-American troops were well across the Elb and feeling for a junction with the Russians. What remained counted only as mopping up. The Panzer war was over.

The war of
the Panzers

On 22nd March, 1945, the Russians had launched an attack along the Küstrin-Berlin Highway. In their path a scratch Panzer division of no name or number prepared for a last stand. It consisted of a reconnaissance platoon with five Panther tanks, a tank company with 22 Panthers and two further companies with 14 Tigers apiece – by comparison a formidable German tank concentration at that late stage in the war and, indeed, just about the only worthwhile mobile forces standing between the Russians and Berlin.

The forthcoming Russian attack, preceded by a 90-minute artillery barrage, followed by massed infantry assault, had many tanks in attendance, but almost at once the German counterfire drove the Russian infantry to ground, leaving some 50 tanks, moving in two columns, to take up the lead and run head-on against two of the German tank companies where they covered the approaches on either side of the highway. Picking their targets, the Tiger and Panther gunners hit and destroyed one attacker

after the other until both prongs melted away. By now the Russians were in some confusion and ripe for counterthrusts launched by the Germans against their southern flank. So far everything had gone in the German's favour, aided by the inept way in which the Russians advanced along the most obvious approaches against an unshaken opponent whose tank gunnery dominated the open landscape.

However, a fresh Russian effort to the north now took gratuitous advantage of the effects of their artillery fire which, by playing on a village where the Germans had kept their Command Post and reserve company, had thrown the reserve into confusion and dislocated control at a critical moment. Laying smoke to cover their assembly and assault, the Russians moved round the flank for the kill, but, in a way, the use of smoke also helped the Germans who managed to reassemble outside the shelled village in the nick of time and open fire on their assailants as they emerged, well silhouetted, from the midst of the

Last battle

The reserve in a village.
A camouflaged Panther

One of the perils of street fighting

Street fighters

smoke screen. The sharp exchange of fire that followed ended, once more, entirely in the German favour and the Russians departed, leaving no less than 60 wrecks upon the field.

This battle at Küstrin may not have been quite the last fought by a Panzer division, but it was certainly one of the last in which a tank force of suitably operational density could be assembled and used with the verve of old. As a reprise, it is a fitting climax to the story of the Panzer divisions and their part in a war dominated by armour and themselves.

What, indeed, was the measure of their achievement, and how did they manage it?

Historical examples illustrating how some brand new mode of warfare has appeared as suddenly and prevailed as thoroughly as did the Panzer divisions in the Second World War, are by no means commonplace. In the past the gradual evolution of weapons and parallel development of tactics permitted contenders to adjust their methods in step with each other so that the superiority of one over another usually remained only marginal. In fact, the victors of the past more often owed their successes to superior training and morale than to technical or tactical advantages. But Panzer divisions epitomised the progressive age in which they lived by succeeding in gathering a new technology and fresh tactics, together with an excellence of training that called, quite deliberately, for a fanatical crusading spirit amongst the soldiers. And all these attributes merged at once just when certain prospective opponents had entered a highly reactionary psychological phase, when most military organisations, numbed by war and economic blizzards, elected to progress with caution and extreme inertia.

Setting aside technological factors, it is still remarkable to record that a comparatively small German Army managed to destroy foes of a strength many times their own, and to persevere in adversity for so long. In the past, many conquering armies, such as those of Genghis Khan, had triumphed by the introduction of superior methods, and, above all, numbers; outnumbered English bowmen had held their ground against superior numbers, not so much by use of their bow as by improved tactics linked with sound training; the Battle Wagon armies of the Hussites in the 15th Century had dominated parts of Bohemia by tactics foreshadowing those of the tank. But not one of these fought with such intensity in a lost cause as did the Panzer divisions, and only the Hussite Battle Wagons evolved with suddenness and enjoyed transitory success.

Panzer divisions did as no other élite has ever done before. They knocked out the most highly rated armies in the world and were robbed of total European domination only by the geographical accident of the sea shielding Britain, the endless steppes comprising Russia, and sheer vastness of the two greatest industrial complexes the world has ever known – Russia's and the combined Anglo-American one. Let it not be forgotten that both Britain and Russia came mighty close to defeat and took over two years to assemble their masses of their own to turn the tables. Remember too that, to within a few months of the final collapse, German Panzer divisions could still rock the Allies on their heels.

In searching for the reasons why the Panzer divisions achieved so much we might, once again, recall the Hussites and ask why they dominated the traditional armies of their day so thoroughly. How did they place their enemies at a severe disadvantage? Fanatical, religious zeal under the direction of a brilliant leader, John Zizka, was certainly one important factor which, linked to their desperation in a struggle for survival, generated a determination similar to that which prompted the German soldiers. But factors such as these have been at work before – and still been partners in defeat – the destruction of the Spartans at Thermopylae, the annihilation of a Roman Legion by Germanic tribes on Teutoberger, and the final defeat of Napoleon's veteran Old Guard at Waterloo, are cases in point where a dedicated élite has died in full flower. It can be seen that the missing link is neither training nor morale – so we are led to suggest that the key element was armoured vehicles.

It was an essential in all infantry battles of the horse and musket age that men should fight shoulder to shoulder in order to concentrate fire of sufficient volume to slaughter a hostile onrush. Unfortunately, infantry found it difficult if not heretical to forsake close order battle drill when faced by the destructive effects of modern arms, since many of their leaders chose to believe, with some reason, that the men drew most courage from close comradeship. After modern weapons had enforced dispersion, the problem of taking measures to sustain the morale of small parties and lonely soldiers loomed large. Naturally, key men who are not easily scared and those who can be trained to resist fear are nature's amplifiers and leaders. But when those leaders become separated from their badly frightened followers the onset of panic is more likely. The perennial communication problem confronting the infantry leader on his feet is how to transmit his will over a wide area to dominate the minds of his men whether they are in sight or not.

Clearly the arrival of tanks upset every battlefield convention in the same way as Zizka's Battle Wagons upset the conventions of warfare in his day. Tanks triumphed, as we have seen, when they operated in a phalanx, at speed and by adopting the least likely line of approach – both physical and psychological. But even when they failed after omitting to obey rules of their own making, the tank crews almost invariably kept on fighting – a trait belonging not only to tank crews, but with the same dedication to the crews of armoured infantry carriers and armoured artillery or assault guns. Thus it is likely that, by being penned inside a steel protective box, fighting men found a new unity in fear even though they fought in small parties.

In an armoured vehicle it is far less easy for the frightened man to give way to his fear. He knows that some-

body in the crew is determined to go on – probably the commander who gives the orders for the rest of the crew to obey – so the driver gets in gear, lets in the clutch and carries them all forward while the remainder of the crew are compelled, whether they like it or not, to fire upon the enemy with their powerful weapons. Thus the armoured vehicle is a mobile cage enclosing courage. And since armoured vehicles, particularly tanks, convey such immense fire-power and give a highly desirable safety to their occupants, the chances of their dominating the enemy are enhanced.

Finally, consider the formidable morale of the German élite who first manned the panzer divisions and, later, the Waffen-SS panzer divisions. That they were an élite was the source of their strength; that such wonderful use was made of their talents is to the credit of men such as Lutz, Thoma, Guderian and Dietrich who organised, formed and trained

them. Written large above their deeds is the spirit that enshrined them – a spirit founded on the comradeship of the vehicle crew, the tactical unity of sections, platoons, companies, battalions, regiments and divisions right up to Army level wherein a special code of communication, partly based on drills, partly on intellect, found transmission in a special jargon that turned the men of a panzer division into something apart from the rest of the German Armed Forces and superior to most opponents.

Never before in history has there been an Army such as that which owed its victories to the German Panzertrupper which, because it was born, grew, fought, and died as an independent Arm of Decision unfettered by outmoded rules and the curbs of the traditional Cavalry, Infantry, and Artillery Arms, instituted a unique brand of armoured warfare that remains, to this day, almost irresistible.

Bibliography

Armour, Richard Ogorkiewicz
Kampfpanzer 1916–66, F M von Senger
und Etterlin
Die Deutsche Panzertrupper,
H Scheibert and C Wagener
The Rommel Papers, ed B H Liddell Hart
Achtung Panzer, H Guderian
Panzer Leader, H Guderian
Lost Victories, E von Manstein
Panzer Battles, F von Mellenthin
The Other Side of the Hill, B H Liddell
Hart
The Tanks, B H Liddell Hart
The Shadow of Vimy Ridge, K Macksey
The Struggle for Europe, C Wilmot
*Purnell's History of the Second World
War*, ed B H Liddell Hart and B Pitt
Various British and US Official Histories
Various documents held in the
libraries of the British Ministry of
Defence and the Royal Armoured
Corps Tank Museum
France 1940, A Goutard
John Zizka and the Hussite Revolution,
Frederick G Heyman